Easy
Money

FINANCIAL TIMES

In an increasingly competitive world, it is quality
of thinking that gives an edge—an idea that opens new
doors, a technique that solves a problem, or an insight
that simply helps make sense of it all.

We work with leading authors in the various arenas
of business and finance to bring cutting-edge thinking
and best-learning practices to a global market.

It is our goal to create world-class print publications
and electronic products that give readers
knowledge and understanding that can then be
applied, whether studying or at work.

To find out more about our business
products, you can visit us at www.ftpress.com.

Easy
Money

HOW TO SIMPLIFY
YOUR FINANCES
AND GET WHAT YOU
WANT OUT OF LIFE

LIZ PULLIAM WESTON

Vice President, Publisher: Tim Moore
Associate Publisher and Director of Marketing: Amy Neidlinger
Executive Editor: Jim Boyd
Editorial Assistant: Pamela Boland
Digital Marketing: Julie Phifer
Publicist: Amy Fandrei
Marketing Coordinator: Megan Colvin
Cover Designer: Chuti Prasertsith
Managing Editor: Gina Kanouse
Copy Editor: Gill Editorial Services
Proofreader: Language Logistics, LLC
Indexer: Erika Millen
Compositor: Nonie Ratcliff
Manufacturing Buyer: Dan Uhrig

© 2008 by Pearson Education, Inc.
Publishing as FT Press
Upper Saddle River, New Jersey 07458

FT Press offers excellent discounts on this book when ordered in quantity for bulk purchases or special sales. For more information, please contact U.S. Corporate and Government Sales, 1-800-382-3419, corpsales@pearsontechgroup.com. For sales outside the U.S., please contact International Sales at international@pearsoned.com.

Printed in the United States of America

First Printing, November 2007

ISBN-10: 0-13-238383-7
ISBN-13: 978-0-13-238383-7

Pearson Education LTD.
Pearson Education Australia PTY, Limited.
Pearson Education Singapore, Pte. Ltd.
Pearson Education North Asia, Ltd.
Pearson Education Canada, Ltd.
Pearson Educatión de Mexico, S.A. de C.V.
Pearson Education—Japan
Pearson Education Malaysia, Pte. Ltd.

Library of Congress Cataloging-in-Publication Data

Weston, Liz Pulliam.

    Easy money: how to simplify your finances and get what you want out of life / Liz Pulliam Weston.
        p. cm.
    ISBN 978-0-13-238383-7 (pbk. : alk. paper) 1. Finance, Personal. 2. Retirement income—Planning. 3. Investments. I. Title.
    HG179.W4753 2007
    332.024—dc22

                                  2007017412

To Will, again and always.

Contents

Acknowledgments

This is yet another book my readers helped write.

Through emails, letters, message board posts, and comments on my blog, readers shared their experiences with money. Their questions, problems, and frustrations vividly demonstrated how complicated our financial lives have become. Their longing for straightforward answers from a source they could trust shaped *Easy Money* into a book that, I hope, provides just that.

As an author navigating the worlds of publishing and publicity, I've benefited enormously from the counsel of three wise women: writers Kathy Kristof, Ilyce Glink, and Dr. Lois Frankel. Thank you all for your generosity, encouragement, and support. I've also been blessed with a string of terrific editors over the years, including Jonathan Lansner, Russ Stanton, Bill Sing, Daniel Gaines, Marty Zimmerman, Richard Jenkins, and Des Toups. Thanks to you, gentlemen.

Then there's the terrific crew at Pearson, including Executive Editor Jim Boyd, Development Editor Russ Hall, Managing Editor Gina Kanouse, and Copy Editor Karen Gill, who almost (*almost*) make book writing fun.

Finally, as always, a big thank you to my husband Will, my best friend and biggest cheerleader.

About the Author

Liz Pulliam Weston is the most-read personal finance columnist on the Internet, according to Nielsen//NetRatings. She's also an award-winning, nationally syndicated personal finance columnist who can make the most complex money topics understandable to the average reader.

She is the author of the national best-seller *Your Credit Score: How to Fix, Improve and Protect the 3-Digit Number that Shapes Your Financial Future* and of *Deal with Your Debt: The Right Way to Manage Your Bills and Pay Off What You Owe*. She also was a contributor to *The Experts' Guide to the Baby Years*.

Liz's columns run twice a week on MSN Money, which reaches more than 12 million readers each month. Millions more read her question-and-answer column "Money Talk," which appears in newspapers throughout the country, including the *Los Angeles Times*, the *Cleveland Plain Dealer*, the *Palm Beach Post*, the *Portland Oregonian*, the *Newark Star-Ledger*, *Stars & Stripes*, and others.

Liz appears regularly on numerous television and radio programs, including American Public Media's "Marketplace Money" and NPR's "Talk of the Nation" and "All Things Considered." She was for several years a weekly commentator on CNBC's "Power Lunch" and has been quoted in numerous publications, including *Consumer Reports*, *Real Simple*, *Family Circle*, *Men's Health*, *Woman's Day*, *Parents*, the *Christian Science Monitor*, the Associated Press, the *Chicago Tribune*, the *Boston Globe*, Forbes.com and others.

Weston is a graduate of the certified financial planner training program at University of California, Irvine. She lives in Los Angeles with her husband and daughter. She can be reached via the "contact Liz" form on her Web site, www.asklizweston.com.

Introduction

Have you paid a late fee on a credit card or bounced a check in the past year? Did you misplace a bill, a statement, or some other financial record that you desperately needed to find? Are you confused about how much insurance you should buy, which health plan you should choose, the right way to save for college or retirement?

Do you ever wish you could spend less time worrying about money?

If so, you're in good company.

People today have to make a lot more financial decisions and keep track of far more details than they did even a generation ago. Instead of one health care plan, you may have to choose from half a dozen—or you may have no insurance at all. Instead of a traditional pension plan provided by an employer, you probably have to save for retirement on your own—and figure out how much to contribute, where to invest the contributions, and eventually how to take your money out. Instead of a credit card or two, you have access to literally tens of thousands of options, all with different rates, terms, and due dates. Even mortgages, which used to come in one basic flavor—fixed rate, for 30 years—have multiplied into a bewildering array of alternatives.

At the same time, the penalties for making mistakes seem to be escalating every day. It's not just that late fees, bounced-check charges, and over-limit penalties are skyrocketing. There are bigger issues. Choose the wrong health coverage, for example, and you could become one of the hundreds of thousands of people each year who have to file bankruptcy, in part because of medical reasons. Mess up on your retirement, and you could be working well past the age when your peers are on the golf course.

If you're like most people, all of this is simply overwhelming. Even if you do have time to research and understand all your options, you probably feel like you don't have time to properly manage every aspect of your finances the way you'd like while still holding down a job, caring for a family, and enjoying a minute or two of leisure time every once in a while.

The good news is that there is hope. You can winnow down your choices, streamline your financial systems, and take control of your money. A few hours spent with this book and a little time invested in today's personal finance technology can put you on track for your goals and alleviate your anxiety about the details that could otherwise trip you up.

Let's get started.

1

Setting Up Your Financial Life

There's a problem with managing your finances the old-fashioned way—it just doesn't work. By the time you get a statement telling you your bank balance, you're already overdrawn by three checks. By the time you get your credit card statement, the thief who has taken over your account has wreaked havoc. Your quarterly 401(k) statements might tell you how some of your investments are doing, but how does that account tie in with your spouse's workplace retirement plan and your IRAs?

And then there are all the fees. Late fees. Over-limit fees. Failure-to-keep-minimum-balance fees. One slip in your money management can cost you plenty.

Monitoring your finances in today's complex world needs to be more real-time. You need to be able to anticipate problems, spot fraud, and move money quickly from place to place as needed.

Fortunately, if you've got a computer and access to the Internet, you've got the tools to simplify, streamline, and safeguard your finances. Do it right, and you'll have a bulletproof system that ensures every base is covered and that significantly reduces your money stress.

Here's what you need to do to get started.

Your Financial Toolkit

The following are essential components for streamlining and simplifying your financial life.

Sign Up for Online Access

Internet access is essential to smart, timely money management. You need to be able to see, 24/7, your balances and recent transactions in your bank, brokerage, credit card, and investment accounts.

Phone access to your accounts is better than nothing, but it's a poor substitute. You'll have to write down balances and transactions rather than being able to see them in front of you. You may also be more limited in how far you can look back; calling up historical information will certainly take more time than if you were using Web access.

Link Your Accounts

Think about how you could get money from one account to another in a hurry. With online access at your bank, for example, you can typically transfer money from savings to checking and back with a few mouse clicks. But what if you need to get cash into the IRA at your brokerage account, and the April 15 deadline is a day away? Your brokerage may offer a service that links electronically to your checking account, making such transfers easy.

Many people link their credit cards to their checking accounts for quick, convenient payments, although the need to do that is lessened if you use online bill paying, as I recommend later.

Allow Your Paycheck to Be Deposited Automatically

Your time is too precious to waste it standing in line at an ATM or teller's window. Besides, it isn't safe to run around with checks or excessive amounts of cash in your wallet. Sign up for direct deposit and have your paycheck safely and automatically plopped into your checking account.

In fact, almost any amount of money you receive regularly is a candidate for direct deposit. You just need the payer to cooperate, and many will, since processing electronic payments is typically a lot cheaper for them than generating and mailing checks.

Set Up Overdraft Protection

Protect yourself from bouncing checks by asking your bank or credit union to set up overdraft protection for your account. With true overdraft protection, money is automatically drawn from a line of credit, credit card, or savings account if you write a check and there's not enough cash in your checking account to cover it. You typically pay an annual fee of $20 to $50 for the service, plus interest on any amounts borrowed. Usually, the total cost is less than one or two bounced checks.

By the way, overdraft protection is different from "bounce protection," which is a different and much inferior service that's offered automatically by many credit unions and banks. With bounce protection, you're allowed to overdraw your account, but the money doesn't come out of your savings or a line of credit. In essence, the bank is lending you the cash but charging you rather hefty fees for the privilege. I've heard from people who have racked up literally thousands of dollars in bounce protection fees in a single year.

Also some financial institutions play dirty by automatically adding the amount of your bounce protection to the balance you see when you check your account at an ATM. The result is that you appear to have hundreds of dollars more in your account than you actually do. This just increases the chances you'll overdraw the account and owe the bank fees.

If your bank is pushing bounce protection, try to opt out in favor of real overdraft protection. If you can't, start looking for another bank.

AN OLD-SCHOOL SOLUTION: PAD YOUR CHECKING ACCOUNT

There's at least one old-fashioned money management tool that still works really well, and that's keeping a pad of cash in your checking account. A *pad* is a sum of money that you leave in your account but don't spend.

Start with $100 and try to build from there. This cushion will help you avoid, or at least reduce, all kinds of bank fees, including minimum account fees and bounced check charges.

Did you know that many banks increase the chances you'll bounce checks by processing the biggest checks first? They say they're doing this to help customers ensure that their most important bills, like rent or a car payment, get paid, but the net result is that you could wind up bouncing more smaller checks and racking up a lot more fees. Let your irritation over this practice motivate you to stymie the banks by keeping a nice pad in your account.

The pad can also bring you some peace of mind. Knowing you always have a few bucks is a lot better than seeing that checking account register empty. This pad will be in addition to the savings you'll do for emergencies and for irregular expenses, which we'll cover in the next chapter.

How do you save to build your pad? Any of the usual budget-shaping strategies will work, such as these:

- Packing your own lunches and snacks
- Making meals rather than eating out
- Eliminating premium TV channels or canceling cable altogether
- Selling stuff in a yard sale or on eBay
- Gathering up your change

How do you keep your pad? Mostly by pretending it's not there. If you use a checkbook or personal finance software to balance your account, you can write a check to yourself in the amount of the pad and never cash it. If it's hidden from you, you're less likely to spend it.

If the only way you track your account is online (or by checking at the ATM), you'll have to mentally erase the amount of your pad from your balance when deciding how much money you can spend.

Open at Least One High-Yield Savings Account That's Electronically Linked to Your Checking Account

You'll want to keep your money working hard for you, and that means getting a higher rate than you'll find at the typical brick-and-mortar bank. You don't have to switch banks, though—just look for an online bank that allows transfers to and from your current checking account.

Three good places to check are ING Direct (http://home.ingdirect.com), HSBC Direct (http://www.hsbcdirect.com) and EmigrantDirect.com. At this writing, all three offer high-rate, FDIC-insured savings accounts with no account minimums and no monthly fees. ING and HSBC also offer free checking accounts that pay a decent interest rate and offer free bill pay; see their Web sites for details.

You may decide to have more than one high-rate savings account to keep track of your money. As you'll read in the next chapter, many people find it convenient to have one account for emergency savings, another for irregular bills, and a third for "fun money." As long as you don't have to mess with account minimums or fees, you can set up as many of these accounts as you like.

Consolidate Your Accounts

Generally, the fewer accounts you have to keep track of, the better.

If you've got 401(k) or other retirement accounts scattered among your last few employers, for example, see if you can roll all the balances into your current plan. If your employer won't allow that, or you don't like the investment choices in your plan, you can roll the balances into a regular individual retirement account (IRA).

If you've got a wallet full of credit cards, single out one or two for everyday use. You needn't close the others—in fact, you probably shouldn't if you're trying to improve your credit scores or if you're in the market for a major loan. But reducing the number of cards you use regularly means you'll have fewer due dates, interest rates, and terms to keep track of. (See Chapter 3, "Get the Most Out of Your Credit Cards," for how to select the best card or cards for your spending patterns.)

Bank and brokerage accounts also tend to proliferate. Ideally, you'd have only one checking account to monitor, but that's not always possible. For some couples, both partners have a separate checking account as well as a joint one. If you run a business, you'll need separate accounts for that. And, as noted earlier, some people really like to open individual accounts when they're saving for specific purposes, such as having one savings account for an emergency fund and another that's dedicated to a future home purchase.

You might be tempted to consolidate all your financial accounts, or at least as many as possible, at one bank or brokerage. Your financial institution would certainly like that; many are trying to capture as much of their customers' money as possible. Banks have brokerage arms, brokerages offer home loans, and everybody's hawking credit cards.

The problem I've always had with the one-stop-shopping approach is that no single financial institution does everything well. Your bank may offer free checking, a nice online bill pay system, and a great ATM network (like ours does), but it may have lousy rates on savings and mediocre rewards programs for its credit cards (like ours does). Your brokerage may offer low-cost access to great mutual funds but too few ATMs and high rates on loans.

Instead of having clear advantages, this kind of consolidation involves compromises, which means there's a cost to you. You might decide to go ahead anyway but remember to review your situation at least annually to see if redeploying some of your accounts elsewhere makes sense.

Consider Two Checking Accounts

I've just said you should consolidate counts wherever possible. Why would you want to turn around and add another checking account?

Several of my readers have told me they struck on this solution after having trouble figuring out how much money in their accounts was available for spending and how much had to be set aside for bills.

The mechanics of the dual checking account system are pretty straightforward. You total up your bills for an entire year, then divide that sum by the number of paychecks you expect to receive (12 if you're paid monthly, 26 if you're paid every other week, 24 if you're paid twice a month and 52 if you're paid weekly). That amount is transferred from your primary checking account to your "bill paying" checking account after every paycheck. (You can do the transfer manually, but I strongly recommend making this automatic.) You then set up your bills to be paid (again, preferably automatically) from this second account.

The money that's left over in your primary account is available to spend on all your variable purchases, such as groceries, gas, clothing, and entertainment.

You should make sure you're getting both checking accounts for free; otherwise, monthly service fees can add up quickly. Your bank may be willing to give you one account for free in exchange for using direct deposit, but may charge you for the second account. If that's the case, you may want to check out the free accounts offered by the online banks mentioned earlier.

The Right Ways to Pay Your Bills

The wrong way to pay bills is willy-nilly, using old-style paper checks and worrying about late fees. The right way includes the steps outlined in the following heads.

Know What You Owe

Take a few minutes to set down, in writing, every bill and obligation you have. Include crucial information like the name of the biller, your account number, the customer service phone number, the payment method you use (such as check, automatic debit, charge to your credit card, online bill pay, etc.), and the bill's due date.

The template on page 8 can get you started. I've left room so that you can add other bills not listed here.

Having all this information in one place can help you in more than one way. It will serve as a checklist as you work through the rest of this chapter, reminding you of what accounts you have and when your bills are due.

But it can also provide crucial information to anyone who may need to take over the finances if you're sick, disabled, or otherwise out of the picture.

In many households, one person does most of the bill paying, and the other family members have no idea what's due when or even which institution to pay. You could avoid a lot of confusion by updating this list occasionally and keeping it in a safe place that's accessible to your spouse, partner, or other trusted person. Just make sure this person knows where to find it.

If you pay your bills online, as I recommend, you'll also want to make a list of all the relevant passwords and keep it in the same safe, accessible place. If someone needs to take over bill paying for you, he or she will need this information to access your accounts.

Set Up a Bill Calendar

You can use a physical, on-the-wall type calendar to write down *all* the due dates for *all* your bills. Or you can use personal finance software like Microsoft Money or Intuit's Quicken; a personal digital assistant (PDA); a smart phone with a calendar feature; or a calendar in your computer. What matters is that you use something you'll actually *see* at least once a week if not more often.

If you take my advice, you'll be using a variety of other methods to make sure all your bills are getting paid on time. Paying bills on time is essential, since one late payment can devastate your credit scores.

Even with those other methods, your calendar is essential. It's your safety net to ensure that none of your bills slips through the cracks. Whatever method you choose, it should be something you consult often and you should include *every* bill, including those that are due annually, twice a year, once a quarter, and every other month.

Bill	Institution	Account Number	Toll-free number	How Paid	Due date?
Mortgage/Rent					
Home equity loan					
Property tax					
Water					
Electric					
Garbage					
Heat					
Other					
TV					
Phone 1					
Phone 2					
Phone 3					
Phone 4					
Internet					
Homeowners Ins.					
Umbrella Ins.					
Auto Ins.					
Health Ins.					
Life Ins. 1					
Life Ins. 2					
Life Ins. 3					
Disability					
Other					
Union dues					
Tuition 1					
Tuition 2					
Student Loan 1					
Student Loan 2					
Student Loan 3					
Credit Card 1					
Credit Card 2					
Credit Card 3					
Auto Reg. 1					
Auto Reg. 2					
Gardener					
Housekeeper					
Babysitter					

CUSTOMIZING DUE DATES

Did you know that if you ask to change your bills' due dates, many companies will comply?

Credit card issuers, phone carriers, utilities, and others are often willing to adjust your due dates if you ask. This can really help you manage your cash flow, particularly if you can spread your biggest bills throughout the month.

Marcia used to struggle because her two biggest expenses— her rent and her credit card bill—came due each month within days of each other. Since she gets paid twice a month, on the 1st and on the 15th, she asked her credit card company to switch her due date to the 20th. Although she still has to keep track of her balances to make sure her other bills get paid, she no longer worries about money being so tight at the start of every month.

Set Up Alerts

I'm a big fan of automatic bill payments, as you'll see later. But there are always some bills that require my attention. To make sure I don't miss one, I've set up alerts on my personal finance software that let me know when various due dates are approaching. You also can set up alerts on your PDA or smart phone, or use an email reminder service (there are a bunch of them on the Web, or check with your Internet service provider) to let you know when bills are due.

Some alert systems go even further. My Discover card lets me know my monthly balance and due date via email; then it sends another email if a payment still hasn't arrived within five days of the due date. Emails also alert me when payments are posted and when my balances reach certain levels. Similar services are available with my American Express card; in addition, the company emails me when "irregular or suspicious" charges show up on my account.

The way you remind yourself isn't as important as making sure you actually do.

Consider Switching to E-Bills and E-Statements

If you really want to cut down on the paperwork cluttering your life, think about switching from paper to electronic bills and statements. You can have them sent to an email account you consult often, so you won't miss anything.

You really don't need the paper as long as you remember to download the statements or bills and back them up occasionally (and backing up your records is something you should be doing anyway). The IRS accepts electronic records, and financial institutions keep your statements on hand for at least six years anyway. (After that point, your chances of being audited are almost nil.)

Many people aren't quite ready to go paperless, though, so I won't insist. Just keep it in mind as an option.

Pay Your Bills Electronically

The check-in-the-mail route is too slow and too unsafe. Your payment is at the mercy of the U.S. Postal Service and the competence of the processor at the other end. If you tell the credit card company you mailed the payment in plenty of time, but the processor insists it didn't arrive by 1 p.m. on the due date (remember, many credit cards have due *times* now as well as due *dates*), who do you think is going to win that argument?

Not to mention how vulnerable check payments are to any thief who's figured out how to raid the mail in transit or at its destination.

And, make no mistake, a paper check is a thief's best friend. Everything he needs to know to invade your account is printed right on the front: your name, address and account number, plus the bank's routing number. A thief might treat the check chemically to alter the Pay To and Amount lines, or he might simply use the check as a template to create bogus ones and write himself a payday.

Contrast that with the typical electronic transaction. The money is transferred out of your account and into someone else's, leaving a clear electronic trail behind. The transactions are encrypted, making them virtually impossible to intercept. And there's usually no question about when a payment was received.

If the recipient is one of the dwindling few that doesn't accept electronic payments, you're still usually better off using an online bill payment system than writing the check yourself.

Here's just one example. Back at the dawn of time, when I was still using lots of paper checks, I wrote and mailed one to a vendor that never made it to its destination. The response from my bank was a metaphoric shrug. The phone rep offered to put a stop on the check for $10 but warned me I'd have to remember to renew it in six months.

Fast forward. I use the same bank's online bill payment system to pay a vendor who doesn't accept electronic transfers, so the bank itself generates and mails the check. Said check never arrives. This time, the bank couldn't have been more helpful. For one, it emailed to notify me that the check hadn't been cashed in a reasonable amount of time. It automatically stopped the check, permanently, for free, and it cheerfully reissued a new one at my command.

I can't guarantee that your bank will be as helpful. But most banks are eager to herd people into electronic payments because electronic transactions are generally cheaper to process than paper ones. That means most banks have a stake in making sure their customers' experiences are good ones.

STAYING SAFE

Some people are reluctant to use online financial services because they fear it makes them more vulnerable to cyber-criminals. In fact, the opposite appears to be true.

People who monitor their accounts online tend to catch fraud and other problems much quicker, according to Javelin Strategy and Research. That helps to stem the damage to an average of $551 per incident, compared to $4,543 per incident for those who waited for statements to come in the mail.

Still, there's no question that establishing online account access gives bad guys a potential route into your finances. But you can do a lot to bar the door. A few basic practices—which you should be doing anyway if you use the Internet at all—will help you keep your finances safer.

Among them:

- **Install a firewall along with antivirus and antispyware programs**—Keep these programs updated and run them frequently.

- **Don't check your balances or otherwise conduct financial transactions on public computers or wireless hotspots**—The free wireless Internet access at your local coffee spot may be a great perk, but it's not secure enough to use for financial transactions. Conduct your financial life on your home computer or at least behind a sturdy firewall.

- **Upgrade to the latest version of your browser**—Some evildoers exploit weaknesses in browsers to do things like divert unwary Internet users to phony bank or credit card sites. Staying up-to-date can help keep you from being a victim.
- **Look for the lock**—Secure financial sites typically start with "https" instead of "http," with the added "s" standing for "secure." They also typically show a little yellow padlock in the lower-right corner of your browser window.
- **Never click on a link in an email or open an attachment you weren't expecting**—The bad guys have gotten awfully good at disguising their emails.

Beware, especially, of *phishing* emails. These purport to come from your bank, brokerage, online auction site, or payment system and warn you of "problems" in your account. You're advised to click on a link in the email, which takes you to a look-alike site whose only purpose is to trick you out of your online ID, password, and other sensitive details. In many cases, these emails are quite authentic looking; the only tip-off you may have that they're not real is that you aren't addressed by name. Even if you're convinced that the email's real, don't respond to it. Instead, call the institution or open a new browser window and type in the address yourself to check your account for messages or problems.

Your goal should be to minimize your use of paper checks, substitute electronic payments, and make your whole system as automatic as possible. You have several options, including these.

- **Online bill pay**—Most banks have online bill payment systems, and they're typically free (or free if you maintain a certain balance). You'll usually find a link to your bank's bill pay system on its home page. Once you sign up, you'll be guided through the easy process of adding companies and individuals to the system so that you can pay them electronically. You can set up recurring payments so your regular expenses that are the same amount, such as your car payment, get sent every month without further action on your part. You also can pay bills manually, which means you specify the amount to be paid each time. Your online bill payment system will tell you

how far in advance you need to initiate payments to ensure
they reach the biller on time. Pay attention to those dates and
consider adding a day or two to ensure every payment gets to
its destination on time.

- **Automatic debits**—Most lenders, utilities, and other regular
  billers offer the option of taking your payment automatically
  from your checking account every month. You still get the bill
  or statement in advance, but no further action is required on
  your part once you've signed up. Some billers, especially
  mortgage and student loan lenders, even give you a break on
  your interest rate for using direct debit. I also like automatic
  debits for credit cards; with it, you can ensure that the minimum payment, *at least*, always gets made on time, and then
  use your online bill pay system to pay off the rest of the bill.
  Finally, automatic payments can be a good solution when the
  amount of the bill varies month to month. If your natural gas
  bill varies from $15 a month to over $200, as ours does, automatic debit makes sure the bill gets covered no matter the
  amount it happens to be that month.

- **Automatic charges to your credit card**—This is a good
  option *only* if you pay your credit card balances in full every
  month and if you make sure you don't max out your card, or
  even come close. If you try it, though, you'll probably love
  the convenience (and potential rewards) of charging bills to
  your credit cards. Instead of a dozen or more separate bills to
  pay, they all come on one statement; if your card offers frequent flyer miles, cash back, or other rewards, you can literally make money by paying your bills. Automatic charges can
  be another good way to pay a bill when the amount varies
  month to month.

You may wind up using a variety of these methods. You may decide, for
example, to put your mortgage and student loans on auto debit to get an interest rate break. You can set your credit cards up for auto debit as well: You'll
have the choice among having just the minimum taken automatically, the full
amount, or a dollar amount you specify. You might even mix it up: choosing
full payment for the cards you use infrequently, which tend to have smaller
balances, and just the minimum on a credit card where you still carry a balance. Recurring and manual payments using your online bill payment system
can cover the rest.

Bill	Best Payment Method
Mortgage	Recurring bill payment (BP) or auto debit
Utilities	Auto debit or credit card
Phone	Auto debit or credit card
Internet	Recurring BP, auto debit, or credit card
Cable/satellite	Auto debit or credit card
Tuition	Recurring BP, auto debit, or credit card
Student loans	Recurring BP or auto debit
Credit cards	Pay minimum with auto debit; pay balance with online BP
Car loan	Recurring BP or auto debit

Build Your Control Panel

Once you've got your financial tools in place, you need to build a control panel so that you can see what's going on with your money *right now*.

I'm a huge fan of personal finance software like Microsoft Money or Intuit's Quicken. I've used financial software for more than a decade, and I believe it's the best way to stay in charge of our money.

At a glance, I can see

- What the balances are in all our accounts as well as what bills are due and how much we'll have left after they're paid

- What we're spending and how each expense category—from auto insurance to vacations—compares to what we spent in a previous period: last month, last year, five years ago

- How well our investments are doing and whether it's time to rebalance our portfolios

- Our progress toward our financial goals and how our net worth has increased over time

Built-in planners help me map out strategies for saving, investing, and paying off debt. Alerts tell me when due dates are approaching or account balances are dipping perilously low (or, in the case of credit cards, when they're getting too high).

The software also keeps track of transactions that affect our taxes. I can easily print reports to take to our accountant or transfer the information to tax preparation software if I wanted to do our taxes myself (which I most emphatically do not).

I can pay bills, move money among accounts, and use our past spending as a template to set up new budgets as needed.

The price for all these benefits? Typically, less than $50 for the software and some time spent setting up your financial accounts so the software can access them. *After that, it takes less than five minutes a few times a week to stay on top of our money.*

With a couple of mouse clicks, I can tell the software to update our balances and record all the transactions that have occurred in our accounts recently. Most of the time, the software can assign categories to those transactions automatically; it knows to put the Exxon Mobile charge into the "Auto:Fuel" category and categorize the Gap purchase as "Clothing."

For all these advantages, though, I realize personal finance software isn't for everyone. The next sections spell out some alternatives.

Account Aggregation 1.0

Some banks, credit unions, and brokerages allow you to view all or most of your accounts on their Web sites—even if the accounts are at other financial institutions.

However, there are drawbacks to these services. You may not be able to add all your accounts. In addition, it can be difficult to project very far ahead to see how your balances might be affected by upcoming bills. Aggregation sites also typically don't have the robust retirement, college savings, and debt payoff planners included in personal finance software. But they're definitely a step up from having to sign on to 3 or 5 or 10 different Web sites to get a complete view of your financial situation.

Account Aggregation 2.0

If you like the idea of account aggregation but your financial institutions don't offer it, or you don't like their set-ups, you have other options. Here are three to check out.

- **Yodlee** provides account aggregation and bill payment services for many big financial companies, but you can also sign up as an individual; it's free.

- **Mvelopes.com** is an electronic version of the old "money envelope" system, where you divide your cash into envelopes for different purposes (groceries, entertainment, gas, etc.). You know at any given moment how much you've spent and how much you have left in each "envelope." The cost is about $8 a month.

- **Wesabe** is a free, community-based Web site where you can not only view all your accounts and track your spending but also tap into the collective wisdom of other users. The "tags" or descriptions you assign to your transactions evoke tips, recommendations, and goals submitted by other people. There are also forums where you can ask for help, share tips, and learn about great deals.

Account Consolidation

Another solution: move all or most of your accounts to a single bank or brokerage. Then your checking, savings, investment, and credit cards will all show up on one Web site.

As I mentioned earlier, you'll probably pay for this convenience. Your bank's investment account fees might be higher than what you'd pay at a discount broker, and its credit cards may not offer the rich reward programs (or low rates) you could find at other issuers. Still, the ability to see your most significant accounts at a glance might be worth the trade-offs.

Excel Spreadsheets

If you're spreadsheet savvy, you can set up Excel to help you track your transactions and account balances. You just have to do a lot of data entry that isn't necessary with Quicken or Money. If you're not a real numbers person, it's easy to fall behind and then feel daunted by the workload needed to catch up. But if you're diligent, you can set up a system that helps you monitor spending, project your cash flow, and track your net worth. You might find Peter G. Aitken's book, *Manage Your Money and Investments with Microsoft Excel*, helpful in getting started.

SHOULD YOU BANK BY CELL?

Many banks now offer the option of using your cell phone to view your balance, transfer money between accounts, or pay bills. You typically use your phone's Web browser, if it has one, or its text messaging system.

Banking by cell is certainly convenient. But is it safe?

The short answer: probably, as long as you take certain precautions.

Most banks don't allow you to do much, yet, with your phone. So, even if a bad guy did steal your phone, or hack into your cell's connection to your bank, the most he'd likely see is your bank balance. His ability to drain your account or even move money around would be pretty limited.

That's not to say there aren't risks. The vast majority of viruses and *malware*—software designed to do bad stuff—targets personal computers rather than phones. But it's not inconceivable that an attack could be directed toward a phone enabled for banking.

So, like most other technological conveniences, there's a risk/reward tradeoff. You can minimize the risks in the following ways:

- Don't download ring tones, photos, video clips, or anything else into your phone from an unknown site. Malware or software viruses could be tagging along.

- If your phone is Bluetooth-enabled, set it to the "non-discoverable" mode. Bluetooth is the short-range network that allows you to use wireless headsets and other devices; you don't want a hacker using it as a route into your phone.

- If you have a smartphone, download and run antivirus software.

- If your phone is lost or stolen, immediately contact your carrier (to shut off service) and your bank (to shut off cell access to your account). Don't store your online ID and passwords on your phone.

Set Up Your Command Center

If you have online access and a laptop, you can theoretically manage your financial life wherever you want. That's especially true if you've ditched paper bills and statements in favor of their emailed counterparts.

Most people, though, are going to want a designated space in their house to process bills, file paperwork, and run their economic ship. The obvious place to create your command center is next to the computer you use to pay bills. If your computer isn't in a good spot, with Internet access and a printer, move it to a place that can accommodate that and the other stuff you're going to need, such as these things.

- **Office supplies**—These include a stapler, paper clips, folders, paper (for writing complaint letters—sometimes you need an actual paper trail), envelopes, pens, stamps, Post-Its, and your checkbook. (We hope you'll soon become like some of my MSN readers, who haven't written a check in years, but until you're entirely comfortable with electronic payments, you may want to keep the paper checks handy.)

- **Tickle file**—Your bill calendar and alerts should prevent a bill from falling through the cracks. But if you're new to electronic payments, or you're still in the habit of being "triggered" to pay bills by the sight of such a bill, you may want to use a tickle file as a back-up reminder. (A tickle file "tickles" your memory about stuff you need to do.) You can use a folder or an accordion file; just make sure you use it *only* for bills, that it's kept separate from other paperwork you need to process, and that you consult it frequently (more about that later).

- **Storage**—Although some people work happily out of a banker's box (those cardboard storage boxes you get at office supply stores), I find it a lot more convenient to have a two-drawer filing cabinet nearby. You may need less space—just a single drawer—if your finances are very simple, if you don't own a business, or if you're in the habit of scanning most of your paperwork and destroying or archiving the originals.

- **A shredder**—As long as you've got paperwork with private personal information—Social Security numbers, account numbers, and so on—you'll need some way to dispose of it safely. Although you can get a basic shredder for as little as $20, you should invest in a more robust crosscut version that shreds more thoroughly and that can dispose of CDs.

- **A filing system**—Although some people are comfortable using a chronological system—filing everything by month, and trusting their memories to recall when something was filed so they can retrieve it—most people will find that an alphabetical system is more intuitive.

  You can divide it any way you like, but some common divisions might include

  - Autos

  - Bank accounts

  - Credit cards

  - Employment

  - Insurance

  - Investments

  - Residence

  - Retirement accounts

  - School

  - Wills and estate plans

You can divide the major headings from there. You'll probably want, for example, separate folders for different kinds of insurance: auto, disability, health, home, life, and personal liability (also known as umbrella coverage).

If you want a terrific ready-made system, let me put in a pitch here for HomeFile, a terrific organizing system created by two financial planners. Not only does it help you make sense of your paperwork, but it also tells you when to discard or archive what. You can find it at the Container Store or at www.homefile.net.

You'll also need some sort of system for handling receipts. Although your transactions will be increasingly handled electronically, you'll still need to track some dead-tree product now and then—for rebates, returns, business expense reimbursements, and the like.

Here's how I do it, using suggestions from Debbie Stanley's excellent book, *Organize Your Personal Finances in No Time*.

Every receipt I get goes into one of three pockets in my wallet, depending on its type:

- **Long-term**—Receipts I need to hold onto for tax purposes or to document big purchases

- **Action**—Receipts I need to submit for business expense reimbursements or rebate offers

- **Short-term**—Receipts I probably will never need again but that I want to keep handy for a few months just in case

Most of my receipts are of the short-term variety, and trying to sort and track them individually is too much of a pain. So I took three folders and labeled them "This Month," "Last Month," and "Two Months Ago." Every few days, I dump a wad of short-term receipts from my wallet to the "This Month" file. At the end of the month, I transfer those receipts to the "Last Month" file. Next month, I'll transfer this batch of receipts to the "Two Months Ago" file. At the end of the third month, I dump the contents of the "Two Months Ago" file in the trash.

I deal with the other receipts in my wallet every week or so—taking action on those that require it and filing the ones I need long term.

This system has served me well. I no longer have to face a mound of unsorted paperwork or a wallet that won't close because it's so jammed with paper. The only things I have to remember are making sure I put every receipt into my wallet (instead of letting the salesperson slip them into the bag, or stuffing them in a pocket) and emptying my wallet into the proper folders every few days.

Staying Up-to-Date

Once you've got your financial toolkit assembled, your bill payment systems locked in, your control panel in place, and your command center set up, you'll probably feel more in charge of your money than ever before.

Let's make sure that feeling lasts. For this system to work, you have to do ongoing maintenance. On a regular basis—at least weekly at first—you'll need to

- Check your bank balances and transactions

- Check your credit card balances and transactions

- Pay any bills that need to go out in the next week (if they're not being paid automatically)

- Update your cash-flow projection (which basically means deducting upcoming bills from your checking account total so you see what you have left to spend)

- Transfer money (if necessary) among your accounts

If your cash flow projection shows that your checking account will be getting a bit low by the end of the week, for instance, you may want to move some money from your savings account. Or if your property tax bill is coming up and you've been saving for it in another account, you'll want to shift that money into checking before sending out the payment.

If you use Quicken or Money, you can probably do all of this in 15 minutes or less. If you have to sign into a bunch of different Web sites and do your projections with a spreadsheet or by hand, you may need 30 minutes or longer at first.

Just make sure to do this update weekly. Set up regular appointments with yourself on your bill calendar, PDA, or other organizing system and make sure not to put it off more than a day or two. Once you're comfortable with the system, you may be able to cut back to every other week or so.

Or you may go exactly the opposite direction. I know some Quicken and Money junkies who update their software daily or even more often. It's actually fun for them to see exactly where they stand. Wesabe tends to have the same effect on folks: many who were clueless about their finances find themselves checking in with their accounts, and their new online money buddies, throughout the day.

You probably have better things to do with your time, but you may understand their enthusiasm when you feel that heady rush of being in control of your money, instead of your money pushing you around, for the first time.

WHEN YOU'RE TRAVELING

Using technology and online tools to manage your money is not just safer, more convenient, and more efficient. It's also a huge relief when you're traveling.

Automatic bill payments ensure that you won't come home to late fees, angry billers, and a dark house because your utilities were cut off. Online bill payment systems allow you to make sure all your other bills are paid while you're on the road. Online account access helps you monitor your bank account and credit card balances. (Just do it safely—don't use public computers or wireless hotspots or type in your account IDs and passwords where anyone else can see them.)

Whether you're traveling on business or for pleasure, you can relax knowing that you haven't forgotten a bill that will make your homecoming miserable.

Your Checklist

Here's your list of things to do from this chapter.

Set up your toolkit.

- ☑ Get online access to your accounts.

- ☑ Link your accounts electronically.

- ☑ Arrange for direct deposit of your paycheck.

- ☑ Set up overdraft protection on your checking account.

- ☑ Open a high-yield savings account.

- ☑ Consolidate redundant accounts.

Set up your bill-paying system.

- ☑ List your bills and due dates.

- ☑ Enter due dates on your bill calendar.

- ☑ Set up due date alerts.

- ☑ Consider using e-bills and e-statements.

- ☑ Choose the electronic payment method for each bill.

Build your control panel.

- ☑ Evaluate your options: personal finance software, account aggregation, account consolidation, Excel spreadsheets.

- ☑ Set up your command center with supplies, a shredder, and a filing system.

- ☑ Schedule weekly financial reviews.

2

Take Charge of Your Spending

Once you've got your financial systems in place, the next step is coming to grips with your spending.

A lot of budgeting advice focuses on the little expenses—the lattes, the dinners out, the ATM fees. The real key to a sustainable budget, though, is in managing the big expenses.

My two favorite budgeting systems acknowledge that fact. They approach the issue of how much to spend in different ways, though, and which you should use depends on how much budgeting help you need.

If you

- Typically get through the month without running out of cash

- Only occasionally get surprised by a big bill

- Usually don't carry credit card debt

- Feel like you're doing okay financially but would like to do better

…then you would probably do great with the 60 percent solution, which was created by MSN Money editor-in-chief Richard Jenkins.

If, on the other hand, you

- Live paycheck to paycheck (or worse, payday loan to payday loan)

- Often run out of money before you run out of month

- Constantly get surprised by big bills

- Have credit card or other high-rate debt

- Have no idea where your money goes

...then you probably need the 50/30/20 plan from *All Your Worth*, an excellent personal finance guide written by bankruptcy researcher and Harvard Professor Elizabeth Warren and her daughter, Amelia Warren Tyagi.

The 60 Percent Solution

Richard Jenkins created this budgeting plan after realizing that his household finances worked best when his family's so-called "committed expenses" were kept to a manageable level. After some experimentation, he decided that level was 60 percent or less of his gross (pretax) pay.

Committed expenses include these:

- Basic food and clothing needs

- Essential household expenses

- Insurance premiums

- Charitable contributions

- All the bills, from electricity to pay TV

- All taxes, including income, property, sales...you name it

The remaining 40 percent is divided so that 10 percent chunks go to the following:

1. Retirement savings

2. Emergency fund savings

3. Short-term savings for irregular expenses like vacations, repairs, new appliances, and gifts

4. "Fun money," which can be spent any way you want

Expense	Monthly Cost	Percent of Gross
Mortgage/rent		
All utilities		
Food		
Clothing		
Household		
Income taxes		
Property taxes		
Insurance premiums		
Child care		
Charitable contributions		
Out-of-pocket medical costs		
Loan payments		
Gas		

To make this budget truly low maintenance, *you need to automate as much of it as possible.* The 10 percent for retirement savings, for example, should come directly out of your paycheck and be deposited into a 401(k), 403(b), or other workplace retirement plan, if available. If you don't have access to workplace plan, you should set up a transfer into an individual retirement account or a brokerage account devoted to retirement.

You can set up other transfers so that the 10 percent for long-term savings and for irregular expenses each go into their own high-rate savings accounts. The 10 percent for fun money can go into another savings account or into a separate checking account, if you decide to maintain more than one.

If you have any bills that are due less frequently than monthly, you should set up an automatic transfer for them as well. These might include property taxes, insurance premiums, auto registration fees, and health insurance deductibles. These can be plopped into your irregular expense fund and drawn upon when the time comes.

Why is automating so important? Because if you have to make a decision each month to transfer the money where it should go, the money might not get there. It's too easy to decide to do something else with it or to fail to take any action at all. By contrast, when the decision is made for you—the money is swept out of your checking account or paycheck with no effort on your part—you don't have to think about it, and you often won't miss it.

WHY YOU NEED AN EMERGENCY FUND

In Chapter 1, "Setting Up Your Financial Life," I told you about the importance of having a cushion for your checking account. Your emergency fund is your cushion for life.

Bad things can and do happen to anyone: job loss, illness, accidents, big unexpected car repairs, a death in the family, divorce. If you're living paycheck to paycheck, you don't have the flexibility to adequately cope. You wind up pulling out your credit cards, adding to your debt woes, or—if your cards are maxed out—you fall behind on your bills, trashing your credit scores and sending your anxiety levels through the roof.

The peace of mind you get from a nice stash of cash, tucked away in a high-yield savings or money market account, is enormous. Once you've built one, you'll never go back to your old living-on-the-edge way of life. It's soooo worth the effort.

How much do you need? Start with a goal of setting aside one week's pay. After that, you may have other financial goals that take precedence for a while, like paying off credit card debt. Once you're able, though, you should start building your emergency fund to equal at least three months' worth of expenses. You can speed things up by tossing in any tax refunds, rebates, or other windfalls.

I'd recommend keeping this money separate from the cash you're accumulating to pay irregular bills, like once-a-year insurance premiums and holiday presents. Don't get in the habit of raiding it for nonemergencies, and it will be there when you really need it.

The money that's left in your checking account is what you've got to pay the rest of your bills. This plan allows you to cover everything—today's expenses as well as tomorrow's—without having to count every penny.

If you can't get those committed expenses under 60 percent, Richard says, it's probably because you've obligated yourself to a more expensive lifestyle than you can actually afford. Maybe your car payment is too high, your mortgage or rent is too expensive, or you've drowned yourself in credit card debt.

You might be able to dig out from the debt by redirecting some of your retirement and long-term savings to that end. You could also fix the issue of too-expensive mortgages and car payments by cutting expenses elsewhere, increasing your income, or both.

But if your committed expenses are well over 60 percent, you're probably having the kind of money problems I mentioned earlier that might make you a better fit for Warren and Tyagi's 50/30/20 plan.

HOW MUCH INCOME SHOULD I COUNT?

Many budgeting systems assume that you'll make roughly the same amount each paycheck. The reality for most American workers is that their paychecks vary from week to week, month to month, or season to season. You might get a lot of overtime one pay period but less or none at all the next; you might be paid on commission or rewarded with bonuses. And some jobs are seasonal; construction workers may pile up the hours in good weather but not work at all in cold or wet times.

When using either the 60 percent solution or the 50/30/20 plan, you'll want to count as income only the amounts *you can reasonably expect to receive* in the coming months. If, for example, you're currently working a lot of overtime but can't count on those extra hours to continue, you might count just your regular pay or try to settle on an average of hours that seems sustainable.

If you work on commission, receive bonuses, have an irregular income, or receive child support from an ex who's a bit of a flake, err on the conservative side when guesstimating what you're likely to receive. (If your ex is a serious flake, you may not want to count on receiving any help at all...at least until the government catches up to him or her.)

However often you get paid—weekly, biweekly, twice a month, monthly—you'll want to come up with an average monthly figure. So multiply your paycheck by the number of paychecks in the year, and then divide by 12.

The 50/30/20 Plan

Richard's plan was based on gross or pretax income. The 50/30/20 plan is geared to after-tax income.

After-tax income isn't necessarily the same as take-home pay, since your employer may well be deducting expenses other than taxes. To calculate your after-tax income, take your gross pay and subtract all the taxes *but not the other deductions,* such as health insurance premiums, parking fees, union dues, or 401(k) contributions.

You'll usually find the taxes grouped together in the same place on your pay stub. Although the abbreviations used vary from employer to employer, they typically include Social Security and Medicare taxes (which may be lumped together as FICA or listed separately as FICA and MEDI, or OASDI and MED or MEDI, or any number of other combinations). They also typically include federal and state income tax withholding, along with contributions to state unemployment and disability funds.

If you've got other income on which taxes will be owed but that aren't withheld, deduct 15–20 percent to come up with an after-tax estimate. Income that falls into this category includes net business income, rents, and royalties. It doesn't include child support that's paid to you, since that's tax exempt.

Now, once you've got your income totals, you can start filling in your must-have expenses. Unlike Richard's committed expenses, these must-haves don't include clothing, miscellaneous household expenses, or charitable contributions, among other common costs.

Instead, you should list the expenses that you currently must pay each month or face serious consequences, such as shelter costs, food, child care and/or private school tuition, utilities (including electric, gas, water, sewage, phone, cell, Internet, and television), transportation (including car payment, auto insurance, maintenance, and fuel), all other insurance premiums, and minimum payments on other loans.

If you pay some of these expenses less often than monthly, you'll want to add up their total annual cost and divide by 12 to get your monthly spending figure. If, for example, you make two property tax payments of $2,400 each, for an annual total cost of $4,800, your monthly spending on that expense would be $400.

To get "percent of after-tax income," just divide each category total by the after-tax income figure you determined earlier.

Your total monthly spending on these categories should equal 50 percent or less of your take-home if you want a sustainable budget.

Ideally, that would leave you 30 percent for your wants—clothes, gifts, vacations, charitable contributions, new furniture, whatever your heart desires—and 20 percent for savings, which would include saving for retirement, building an emergency fund, and paying off any high-rate debt, like credit cards.

If you've totaled your must-haves and they're waaaaay over 50 percent—well, you've got plenty of company.

Category	Monthly Spending	Percent of After-Tax Income
Mortgage or rent		
Property taxes		
Utilities		
Food		
Child care/tuition		
Transportation		
Medical premiums and deductibles		
Other insurance premiums		
Loan payment #1		
Loan payment #2		
Loan payment #3		
Loan payment #4		
Loan payment #5		
Total:		

I recently heard from one young man who was struggling to understand why his family couldn't make it on $40,000 a year. It turned out that his must-have expenses totaled nearly 90 percent of his after-tax income.

His housing costs gobbled up nearly 40 percent of his net pay. His car chomped another 20 percent—and that was before considering fuel costs, repairs, or maintenance. Health insurance premiums consumed an additional 15 percent.

For comparison, credit counselors typically recommend you spend no more than a third of your pay on housing expenses, and they worry if you're spending more than 10 percent on health insurance and related costs. How much you should spend on cars varies by how much you pay out in other categories, but for many families, 10 percent might be too high.

Now, this guy had good reasons for all his spending choices. He needed the car to get to work, and it wasn't a very expensive vehicle—he wound up with a very high interest rate because of past money troubles. He didn't want to move his family to cheaper, less desirable housing, and he wanted to maintain his more flexible health insurance rather than settle for HMO coverage.

Good reasons don't change the math, though. If your must-have expenses claim too big a chunk of your income, you can't have a comfortable financial life. You can't save enough for retirement or for emergencies; you'll always end up scrambling at the end of the month; and you're in grave danger of digging a serious debt hole from which you won't emerge unscathed.

The math also doesn't change if you live in a high-cost area, and the answer isn't complaining that everything's too expensive. If you want a manageable financial life, you need to reduce those big budget-killing expenses, trim like mad everywhere else, make more money, or move to a more affordable area...or some combination of these.

Yes, it would be nice if somebody fixed the health care crisis, expanded the supply of good inexpensive childcare, made housing in decent school districts affordable for all families, and reined in the credit card companies and other lenders. I just don't think we can count on any of those things happening in the near future and maybe not in our lifetimes. We're on our own, and those who don't face the reality of the math are the ones in danger of being bankrupted by it.

Now, you may be able to get by *temporarily* with must-haves that exceed 50 percent, such as in these situations.

- You're adjusting to a new child or a breadwinner is disabled or laid off.

- You've overcommitted to a house or car payment, a situation that may take months or years to fix.

- You've decided you're willing to make sacrifices necessary to keep your child in private school or in the too-expensive day care.

In these situations, the money for these extra must-haves needs to come out of the wants category rather than the savings portion. You'll need to take cheaper vacations or stay at home; forgo new clothes or buy them sparingly; skimp on charitable donations; or put off those home upgrades you've been wanting to do.

If financial peace of mind is important to you, though, eventually—and better sooner than later—you need to get your expenses in line.

It helps to have the right attitude. The words *won't* and *can't* should be removed, at least temporarily, from your vocabulary. You'll need to take a look at each spending category with the clearest possible eyes and see where trimming is possible.

You can find plenty of money-saving ideas on the Web and at the library, so I won't go into exhaustive detail here. You may find potential solutions in the list that follows, or you may not; these suggestions are meant to start you thinking about the possibilities.

- **Housing**—Get a roommate or a boarder; refinance your mortgage; move.

- **Property taxes**—Appeal your assessment to the county tax collector if it's too high.

- **Utilities**—Turn your thermostat down in the winter and up in the summer; use shades and blinds to manage the sun's heat; replace regular light bulbs with compact fluorescents; take shorter showers; run the dishwasher, washing machine, and dryer only when they're full; use a drying rack instead of the clothes dryer; use a prepaid cell phone; trade your land line for a cell or use Internet calling; drop high-speed Internet access, premium TV channels, or cable altogether.

- **Food**—Bring lunches and snacks to work; make meals at home rather than dining out or calling for delivery; make more meatless meals; plan meals according to grocery schedules; buy in bulk; plant a garden; use food banks or apply for food stamps if money is extremely tight.

- **Child care**—Parents want the best care possible for their children, and there's not enough affordable quality care available. That said, you should at least explore your options if you're having money problems. You may find a more affordable day care that's as good or better than the one you have now or qualify for government-supported services you didn't realize were available (visit www.govbenefits.gov for details). If your child has been used to one-on-one care, you may be able to share the costs of a nanny with another family or find a reasonably priced in-home service with just a handful of kids. You may even discover that staying at home is a good option for you or your partner, particularly if you're losing ground financially by working once child care, taxes, commuting, and other costs are considered.

- **Transportation**—Sell a car; drive less by car pooling, taking public transportation, and making fewer trips; use car share services like FlexCar or ZipCar; increase your insurance deductible; shop for cheaper coverage; make sure you're getting all the discounts you're entitled to; drop comprehensive and collision coverage on older cars.

- **Medical expenses**—Switch from traditional or preferred provider coverage to HMO; consider a high-deductible plan; investigate health savings accounts; if you don't have insurance, negotiate directly with doctors and hospitals for lower fees and use low-cost or free clinics where possible.

- **Other insurance**—Raise deductibles; shop for cheaper coverage; drop unneeded policies.

One other thing: don't dismiss the idea of making more money as the solution to your money issues. Sometimes that's the best way out of a jam. I've heard from lawyers who moonlighted on freight loading docks, stay-at-home moms who started day care centers, and people who launched paying Web sites in their spare time. You'll want to avoid get-rich-quick schemes and any business, venture, or job that requires a big up-front investment, but if you look around, you're likely to find plenty of other possibilities for boosting your pay.

TRY A BUY-NOTHING MONTH

The usual advice when you're not sure where all your money goes is to keep a notebook handy and write down every expense for a month or so. That approach helps identify the little "leaks" in your budget, such as the $2 a day you're spending at the vending machine or the $30 you blow on a night at the movies.

Here's another, more radical approach: Try a buy-nothing month. Resolve to spend money only on absolute necessities: gas for the car, diapers for the baby, and perishables like milk, fruit, and vegetables.

With everything else, it's "use it up, wear it out, make it do, or do without." You'll raid your pantry and freezer to make all your meals at home. You'll take lunches and snacks to work and have picnics instead of using the drive-through. You'll entertain yourself with library DVDs and books. You may even have to give yourself a haircut, or just be a little shaggy for a month. Dozens of readers of the "Your Money" message board on MSN volunteered to try a "Buy Nothing" month during February 2007, and many said it was a transformative experience. They learned when they were spending out of habit or boredom, and the average amount saved that month was around $400.

The buy-nothing month accomplishes several goals at once.

- You'll get a real feel for the difference between needs and wants.
- You'll get creative about finding solutions to everyday dilemmas when you can't just buy a solution.
- You'll identify plenty of areas in your budget where you can cut back.
- You'll save a pile of money.
- You'll really, really enjoy that latte or dinner out when you can finally indulge again.

Once you've got your basic budget worked out on the 50/30/20 plan, you can start automating your choices the same way you would under the 60 percent solution.

- At least 5 percent and preferably 10 percent should go directly from your paycheck into retirement savings; the rest of the 20 percent can be directed to paying off credit card and other high-rate debt if you have it or for building up your emergency fund if you don't.

- Transfer the 30 percent for your wants into your high-rate savings account. You can move it with a click of your mouse into your checking account, as needed.

- Transfer the amounts needed to cover less regular expenses, such as property taxes or annual insurance premiums, into a separate high-rate account. Total all these expenses to see how much you spend annually, divide by 12, and move that amount monthly into this second account.

- The rest of the money in your checking account will be devoted to bills.

With either of these spending plans, there will be some trial and error. You may discover an expense you'd forgotten about, and your bills will certainly change over time. Fortunately, both these plans are flexible. As your finances become more manageable, you won't have to worry about every penny since the dollars will be taking care of themselves.

These plans also will help you figure out what you can afford when it comes to future bills and loans. If you're in the market for a car, for example, you'll know that you can really afford the payment if, combined with your other bills, the new payment and insurance costs don't push committed expenses over 60 percent of your gross pay (under Richard's plan) or your must-haves over 50 percent of your after-tax pay (under the Warren plan).

KNOWING HOW MUCH YOU CAN SPEND

If you take my advice to use personal finance software, such as the latest versions of Microsoft Money or Intuit Quicken, you'll always know where you stand financially. These programs have cash flow features that tell how much you have left over to spend each month once all your bills are paid.

If you decide not to use the software, you'll need to do the cash flow projections yourself. You can use a spreadsheet, if you're comfortable using those, or just employ pencil, paper, and calculator.

First you'll log the income you expect to receive in the coming month. Then you'll write down the bills that need to be paid, their due dates, and how much you'll have left over after they're paid.

Here's an example of a cash flow projection created by a young renter who's paid twice a month and who's roughly following Richard's 60 percent solution.

She makes $35,000 a year and contributes 10 percent off the top to her 401(k) plan. Another $6,000 or so goes to various taxes. After employer deductions for basic health insurance, her net check is about $1,000, and she's paid twice a month.

Her biggest fixed expenses—rent, student loan payment, utilities—come due early in the month. To keep from experiencing a money crunch every month, she asked her other billers—her auto insurer, phone company, and Internet provider—to move their due dates to the end of the month. That's also when she transfers money to cover her irregular expenses and "fun money" and to build up her emergency fund.

Currently, her committed expenses are above Richard's 60 percent limit. To compensate, she's reduced her "fun money" and the amount that goes to irregular expenses. Fortunately, she has very few—all her bills are due monthly, and she just needs to save a little extra for gifts and travel.

	When due	Amount	Balance
Paycheck #1	1-May	$1,000	$1,000
Rent	1-May	($500)	$500
Student loan	8-May	($200)	$300
Utilities	10-May	($100)	$200
Paycheck #2	15-May	$1,000	$1,000
Auto insurance	20-May	($75)	$925
Phone/Internet	23-May	($100)	$825
Irregular bills	20-May	($100)	$725
Emergency fund	22-May	($350)	$375
Fun money	23-May	($100)	$275

Once she records her income and expenses, she knows how much money she has to spend on variable expenses like food, gas, and clothing. For the first 15 days of the month, for example, she has $200 for those costs (which is the balance she'll have on May 10, after her rent, car payment, and utilities are paid). For the last half of the month, money will be a bit less tight; she'll have $275.

As long as she takes the time to write down each month's income and expenses in advance and keep a running tally, she'll know exactly how much she has to spend.

How Do I Prioritize My Goals?

A reader of my newspaper question-and-answer column emailed me in frustration. Most of the articles he read on personal finance seemed to assume that the particular issue under discussion—whether it was saving for retirement, paying off debt, accumulating an emergency fund, saving for college, or buying insurance—was the reader's only priority, or at least his most important one.

But in the real world, he pointed out, people have to juggle their priorities. They may not have enough money to save the optimum amount for retirement while paying off their cards, saving a pile for emergencies and college, and loading up on insurance.

How do you decide what comes first?

My previous book, *Deal with Your Debt*, goes into detail about how to figure out your priorities. Typically, you'll be trying to achieve more than one goal at a time, and how many you can tackle will depend on your available funds. For most people, though, it should go something like this:

1. **Save for retirement**—I like to see people putting aside at least 10 percent of their incomes, and preferably more, for their later years. You may be able to reduce this percentage if you're already vested in a generous traditional pension—the kind that will replace a majority of your income in retirement. Otherwise, you'll need to build to this level of savings as quickly as possible. Retirement savings isn't optional or something you should put on hold.

2. **Build a small pad**—Getting at least a few hundred dollars in savings will help you absorb unexpected expenses. You typically don't need to focus on building a large emergency fund—the kind meant to cover 3 to 6 months' worth of expenses—until you've met other goals.

3. **Pay off toxic debt**—If you have credit card balances or owe money to payday lenders, you need to get rid of that debt fast. If your debt is of the nontoxic variety—like most mortgages, home equity loans, student loans, and auto loans—then paying it off rapidly doesn't need to be a priority.

4. **Review your insurance**—You'll find Chapter 6, "Insurance: Protecting What You Have—and Will Have," is devoted to this topic, but after making sure you have adequate home-owners and auto insurance, you need to assess your needs for health, life, and disability insurance, usually in that order.

These are the "First Four" priorities of financial planning. But they probably won't be the last.

Once you've covered the First Four, you may still have more prioritizing to do. You may want to get to work on building that emergency fund or saving for a down payment on a house if you're not already a homeowner. If you have kids, you probably should get a college fund started. You may have other goals: a special vacation abroad, home improvements, a car. You may want to pay down home equity lines of credit or even the mortgage itself.

How you order those goals, though, is up to you, your values, and your circumstances. As long as you've covered the First Four, you should be in pretty good financial shape.

Couples and Money

There's no one right way for couples to handle money. You don't have to do it the way your parents did, or the way your friends do, or the way you did it during your first marriage. What's important is creating a system that works for the two of you now, as a couple.

Some spouses put their money into a combined pot. Others keep strictly separate accounts, carefully dividing up the household bills. Some combine the approaches, with a joint account for most expenses plus individual accounts for "mad" money.

However you decide to divvy up the accounts and the bills, though, certain approaches do tend to work better for most people. Such as:

- **Let one person handle the bills**—One of you is bound to be at least a little better at bill-paying, and it's much simpler to have one person in charge than to try to rotate the duties or divide up who pays what. It's smart to create a folder of information the other partner may need to take over bill-paying in an emergency, but otherwise it's easier to have one Chief Financial Officer.

- **Have private funds**—Some couples are perfectly content sharing everything, but if fights over money are an issue you might want to consider a system where each of you gets some money to spend with no questions asked. How much depends on your budget and circumstances, but even a few bucks a week to blow on lattes or a movie can be enough to preserve a necessary sense of independence.

- **Don't have secrets**—Having a bit of "no questions asked" money is one thing. Hiding money, purchases, or debts from your partner is quite another. You may dismiss these issues as no big deal, or even necessary to avoid fights, but in reality they're a kind of financial infidelity that can cause serious problems in your relationship. Few secrets stay that way for long, particularly when money is involved; if your partner feels deceived, your marriage could pay. The better course is to be honest with each other: no "little" secrets, no unpleasant surprises.

- **Set a ceiling**—You also can head off a lot of money battles simply by agreeing not to make purchases above a certain dollar amount without consulting your significant other. The actual limit can, again, vary by your budget or circumstances. It might be $20, or $200, or (if you're really well off) $2,000. What's important is that you both agree to the limit and talk before you spend more.

- **Respect your partner's trigger points**—My friend Nicki was fuming after another money fight with her husband. She'd purchased a bunch of clothes on the same day that a payment for a particularly large credit card bill cleared their bank. The transactions delivered a one-two punch that almost completely drained their checking account—and it wasn't the first time something like this had happened. Nicki's husband was furious, but so was Nicki. It wasn't as if they were broke or couldn't afford the clothes, Nicki protested, and her husband even knew that she planned on shopping that week. Why couldn't she just dip into their savings and tell him to get over it?

  Well, I knew why. As a fellow "hoarder," I understand her husband's gut-level conviction that the savings account is sacred territory—there for emergencies only. "If you want to keep him happy," I suggested, "make sure there's *always* money in the checking account." Seeing a checking account on fumes or having to dip into savings to cover bills is the surest way to send a hoarder into panic, no matter how temporary the situation might be.

  This little insight into how the hoarder's mind works was all Nicki needed. She realized that most of their bills were due around the first of the month, which created a cash-flow crunch. They always had plenty of money at the end of the month, when their account was brimming with their paychecks and no bills were due. So she moved some of their big bills to the second half of the month. She also started keeping an eagle eye on their checking and credit card balances to make sure she always knew where they stood. The result: *a happier couple*.

- **Compromise, compromise, compromise**—Now a word to my fellow hoarder/saver types: wipe that self-righteous smirk off your face. Because we tend to be good with money—or at least better at handling it than our spender-type partners—we can sometimes slip into thinking that our way is the only right way to be. Instead of talking *with* our partners about goals and spending, we can be guilty of lecturing *to* them. No one wants to be treated like a child, though, and it's often counter-productive: your partner either tunes you out or goes out to spend more in an "I'll show you!" huff. Hoarder or saver types also need to understand, and compromise with, their "spender" partners. Someone who likes to dress well, eat out, or shop for entertainment isn't going to suddenly give all that up overnight—at least not happily. Unless your finances are already in crisis, the saver should try to make sure the budget includes money for purchases the spender believes are impor-tant, even if that means somewhat slower progress toward your other financial goals.

- **Check out a few books about couples and money**—Books specifically devoted to this topic can give you valuable insights about how to work with a partner to develop a sound financial plan. A good one is David Bach's *Smart Couples Finish Rich*. If there's a spender in your relationship, Olivia Mellan's *Overcoming Overspending: A Winning Plan for Spenders and Their Partners*.

- **Get help if you need it**—Money is far from easy for many couples, and sometimes the conflicts run so deep that profes-sional counseling is needed. An investment in couple's ther-apy could pay off in a happier marriage and greater economic prosperity once the two of you are rowing your boat in the same direction, instead of fighting each other for control of the oars.

IMPULSE SPENDER? CREATE A "PAUSE" BUTTON

If you have trouble controlling your spending, you might benefit from what technique therapists recommend for their clients with attention deficit or impulse control disorders: creating a mental "pause" button.

Folks with these disorders often don't think before they act. In a store or online, they may buy impulsively without reflecting about whether they can really afford the purchase. Their knee-jerk response, according to Debbie Stanley, professional organizer and author of *Organizing Your Personal Finances in No Time*, is "It's so cool, it's right here, and if I don't buy it now I know I'll forget about it!"

Inserting a pause between the impulse to buy and the actual purchase may be all they need to short-circuit a budget-busting shopping spree. Some ways to do that:

- **Carry a list of "things to buy."** This can be a sheet of paper or notebook you carry in your wallet or purse or a virtual list loaded on your smartphone. If you see something you think you want, don't buy it right then—just add it to the list. "In this way, you can capture the idea without wrecking your budget," advises Stanley.

- **Have a waiting period.** A three-day "cooling off" period is good, although some people find three weeks is even better. Chances are the thing that initially appeared cool and essential will seem a lot less so on reflection. If you still decide you want to buy it, you can research your options for getting the best deal.

- **Shop with a list**. Don't use this list as a guideline; treat it as set in stone. If something's not on the list, don't buy it; you can add the something to your list of "things to buy" on a return trip.

- **Check your balance.** Before you approach the check-out counter in a store or online, call your bank or visit its Web site to review your account balance. If you're planning to use a credit card, make a second call to the issuer to check your balance there as well. These reminders can keep you from indulging in an "I'll think about it tomorrow" haze that can lead to big credit card bills and bounced checks.

Your Checklist

Here's your list of things to do from this chapter:

See where you stand.

☑ Figure out your average monthly income.

☑ Determine your average spending in each budget category.

☑ Calculate what percentage of your income is spent in each budget category.

Choose your budgeting options.

☑ Use the 60 percent solution if your budget's basically in good shape.

☑ Opt for the 50/30/20 budget if you're struggling.

☑ Look for ways to cut expenses.

☑ Automate your savings for retirement, emergencies, and irregular bills.

If you're part of a couple:

☑ Select a Chief Financial Officer to pay bills.

☑ Determine how much "no questions asked" money each partner will get weekly.

☑ Set a "talk to me" ceiling for purchases.

3

Get the Most Out
of Your Credit Cards

Some people believe that credit cards are evil by nature. And they have a point.

By offering substantial credit limits and small minimum payments, credit cards encourage people to pile up debt that becomes harder and harder over time to repay. Interest rates tend to be high and can shoot even higher when people skip payments, max out their cards, or miss a payment to another creditor.

I've heard from hundreds of people over the years who viewed their credit cards as sleeping snakes in their wallets that one day rose up to bite them.

For most people in the 21st Century, though, credit cards are a great convenience. They can help you build your credit rating, bail you out in a crisis, and even help your bottom line through rewards programs.

Whether cards become your friends or your foes depends on how you handle them. And the game plan differs depending on whether or not you carry a balance. If you do carry a balance, continue reading. If you don't, you're already ahead of the game and can skip to the second section.

If You Carry a Balance

Despite what you may have heard, carrying a big credit card balance isn't the norm in America. Federal Reserve statistics show

- One quarter of U.S. households don't have credit cards.

- Another 30 percent or so pay their balances in full every month.

- Of the remaining 45 percent, half carry balances of less than $2,200.

- Only 1 household in 14 has more than $10,000 in credit card debt.

- Only 1 household in 50 has more than $20,000 in credit card debt.

Obviously, statistics that purport to show the "average" American carrying $9,000 or more in credit card debt are misleading. These figures typically take all the money owed on credit cards at the end of the year and divide them by the number of households that have at least one card. The statistics don't correct for the fact that many of the balances owed on Dec. 31 will be paid off the next month. They also don't compensate for the fact that the big balances owed by a few are skewing the average for the many.

So if you've ever taken comfort in the fact that your credit card balances weren't that bad compared to the rest of the country—sorry. Any balance is bad for your financial health, and the bigger the balance, the more out of step you are with your peers.

What's more, carrying a balance leaves you vulnerable to all kinds of credit company tricks, such as these:

- **Universal default penalties**—It makes sense that credit card companies will increase your rate if you fall behind on your payments. You've clearly become a bigger risk. But many issuers regularly cruise your credit reports looking for evidence you're falling behind and will boost your rate if they discover you've been late with any *other* creditor. This "universal default penalty" means you can be punished even if the problem wasn't your fault, such as when your insurer fails to pay a medical bill and it goes into collections.

- **Double-cycle billing**—This is a particularly nasty practice that involves charging you interest for two months even when you carry a balance for only one.

- **Bait and switch**—A number of credit card companies don't tell you what interest rate you'll get until after you've applied and been approved for a card. You may think you're applying for a low-rate balance transfer offer, but you may get approved for a card with a much higher rate and worse terms.

The good news is that you don't have to live with these tactics. Plenty of people have dug themselves out of serious credit card debt. One of my favorite examples is Mary Hunt, a Southern California woman who paid off more than $100,000 in unsecured debt over 13 years. She began sharing what she learned about saving money in her "Cheapskate Monthly" newsletter, which has since grown into an empire that includes a Web site, www.DebtProofLiving.com, and several books, including *Live Your Life for Half the Price*.

There are lots of other examples, including these:

- Wanda, a New Mexico attorney who in her late 40s took a second job on a freight-loading dock to torpedo $25,000 in credit card debt in one year

- Greg, a Delaware man who eliminated $35,000 in debt in less than a year

- Glori, an Arizona musician who paid off about $30,000 in debt in 18 months on an annual income of $40,000

How did they, and the hundreds of others who shared their debt-reduction stories with me, do it? Each took a slightly different path, but they also had much in common. They

- **Eliminated the words *can't* and *won't* from their vocabularies**—Many people stall out in their efforts to save money and reduce debt because of expenses they think they can't live without. In reality, we can do without a lot of things. You won't have to live like a monk forever, but being willing to do so for short periods can really help speed you to your goal.

- **Reviewed every expense and were brutal about trimming every way they could**—Nothing should be off-limits. Whatever the expense, there's a way to reduce it. You can get ideas from Web sites like Mary's or The Dollar Stretcher (www.stretcher.com) and from the frugal-living books at your local library.

- **Looked for ways to boost their income, even though it meant longer workdays**—Wanda worked from 6:30 p.m. to 8:30 p.m. at the dock on weekdays; Greg volunteered for overtime at his main job and took on a second job as well; Glori got an insurance license, tutored students, and taught at a local college.

- **Often used cash to restrict their spending**—For most people, electronic transactions—credit cards, debit cards, electronic payments, and so on—are the way to go. If you're on a strict budget, though, you may find using actual cash really helps you stay on the straight and narrow. Joy, a Washington state woman who paid off $8,000 in eight months, gave herself $150 a month in cash to cover all her variable expenses like food, gas, and entertainment. Others divvy amounts of cash into different envelopes for different purposes. Either way, when the money's gone, it's gone—no going back to the ATM to get more.

Here's a game plan to help you eliminate your credit card debt.

- **Stop using the cards**—This is the nonnegotiable first step. You really do have to put the cards away so you're not adding to the already-considerable pile. You can live without them for now. The one exception: if you travel for business and get reimbursed by your company, you obviously will need to keep using that card. Otherwise, it's cold turkey time.

- **Make a budget**—Identify the places you can cut and the ways you can raise money. Write your budget down so you have a guide and something to compare against your actual spending.

- **Negotiate with your credit card companies for lower rates**—You'll have the best chances of success if you're a good, on-time customer and your FICO credit scores, which range from 300 to 850, are 700 or above. (If you don't know what your FICOs are, invest about $50 to buy them and your credit reports from MyFico.com. You're entitled to free annual credit *reports* from www.annualcreditreport.com, but credit *scores* aren't free, and the ones you're pitched at the free report site generally aren't FICOs, which are the scores most lenders use.)

Next, gather some competing offers. You may be receiving low-rate balance transfer offers in the mail, or you can see current offers at sites like CardRatings.com and Bankrate.com. How low are the rates? How long do these low rates last before they expire? Pick the best offers and prepare to use them as leverage with your company.

Now call up your credit card company. Point out that you're a good customer and that you're considering a competitor's offer. Ask the phone representative if she can lower your rate.

If you're a good customer, the card company will probably give you at least some kind of break. After all, it costs them about $200 to recruit new customers, said CardRatings.com's Curtis Arnold, so most are eager to hang on to the ones they've got.

If the interest rate reduction isn't as much as you'd hoped, you can play hardball by saying "Thanks, but no thanks—I think I'd like to close my account now." You shouldn't really go through with this threat—closing accounts can hurt your credit scores—but those words should help get you transferred to the customer retention department, which is usually much more able to wheel and deal than the frontline phone reps.

If you still don't get a better deal, you can always use one of those competing offers to transfer your balance. This is usually a second rather than a first choice, since most transfer offers tack on 3 to 4 percent fees that increase your debt and offset some of the savings. Also opening a new credit card account can ding your credit scores. But the interest savings may be worthwhile and could help you speed up your debt repayment.

If you choose a balance transfer, be sure to do the following:

- **Read all the fine print—twice**—These deals can be spring-loaded with traps to catch the unwary. In addition to the fees you may be charged, you should be especially careful to understand what the interest rate is, exactly how long it lasts (in other words, the exact date the low or "teaser" rate expires), and what can trigger a higher rate. Many cards will raise your rate if you're late with a single payment or if you fall behind with any other creditor.

- **Pay early**—Set up automatic payments, and make sure the payments arrive several days in advance of the due date to ensure you don't lose your great rate.

- **Put the card on a shelf**—Once you've transferred a balance, don't use the card again until the balance is paid off. New purchases and cash advances will accrue at a much higher interest rate, and your payments will be used to pay down the low-rate balance transfer *first*, which means you'll wind up paying those high interest rates for months.

If your credit scores aren't good, you may have other options to lower your interest rates. You may be able to borrow from your 401(k), take out a home

equity loan or line of credit, or get a debt consolidation loan. These choices
are filled with peril, however.

- The biggest danger with a 401(k) loan is that you might
  lose your job and have to pay back the balance in a hurry
  or risk having it taxed and penalized as a withdrawal.

- Home equity borrowing puts your home at risk and turns
  what should be short-term debt into potentially long-term
  debt. Your home equity generally should be reserved as a
  financial cushion, not squandered away on meals, vacations, clothes, and other fleeting purchases.

- The debt consolidation world is filled with companies that
  charge big fees for loans that may not save you much and
  could even cost you more in the long run. If you belong to
  a credit union, check there to see if you can get a personal
  or debt consolidation loan that makes sense. Otherwise,
  it's best to skip this option.

Another danger with all these options: you may not fix the spending problem
that got you into debt in the first place. A lot of people who use these quick
"fixes" simply run up more credit card debt. If you use any of these fixes, make
them real, one-time-only solutions by getting your spending under control.

If you are really up to your ears in debt, you should consider the
following:

- **Talk to a credit counselor**—If you've fallen behind on your
  credit card payments and can't seem to catch up, you may be
  a good candidate for a credit counselor's debt management
  plan.

  These plans allow many borrowers to avoid bankruptcy by
  reducing their credit card interest rates and putting them on a
  payment plan that allows them to retire their debt in a few
  years.

  Debt management plans aren't for everyone, and they're particularly not for those who can figure out a way to pay off
  their debts on their own. Although participation in such a
  plan is considered a "neutral" by the leading credit scoring
  formula—neither good nor bad for your credit scores—your
  current lenders may punish you by reporting you as late,

which *would* hurt your scores. In addition, prospective lenders may shy away from you until you've completed the plan.

Also you have to choose your counselor carefully. This industry got a huge black eye in the 1990s when it was overrun by a bunch of scam artists and for-profit companies masquerading as nonprofits. The Federal Trade Commission and the IRS finally caught on to the magnitude of the problem and started acting against some of the worst offenders.

You'd be smart to pick an agency that's affiliated with the National Foundation for Credit Counseling, the oldest and most respected group. You can find them at www.nfcc.org.

• **Talk to a bankruptcy attorney**—Most people rightly want to avoid bankruptcy, but sometimes it's the best of bad options. If repaying your credit cards, medical bills, and other unsecured debts will take you more than five years, you might want to at least consult with a bankruptcy attorney about your options. Bankruptcy will be a devastating blow to your credit history, but it's one that people can recover from if they learn their financial lesson and start using credit responsibly.

Zero Percent Jockeys

Most folks who carry big credit card balances lose tons of money every year in finance charges. But a handful of people actually make money from their debt.

These folks take advantage of the difference between the lower rates some credit cards offer on balance transfers and the higher rates available from online savings accounts. I call them credit card arbitragers, since *arbitrage* means taking advantage of a disparity in prices or interest rates.

Here's how it works. Folks who have excellent credit and big credit limits (typically $10,000 or more on each credit card) scour their mail and online forum sites like FatWallet.com looking for special 0% balance transfer offers. These offers must

• **Have no or limited balance transfer fees**—The typical balance transfer offer tacks on a 3 percent or 4 percent fee, which would wipe out any benefit from the scheme. If the arbitragers can't find a no-fee transfer, they look for one that caps the fee at $75 or so.

- **Not restrict how the money can be used**—The vast majority
  of balance transfer offers require the borrower to use the
  money to pay off another credit card. But arbitragers look for
  offers that allow them to write a check to themselves or have
  cash wired from the credit card company into a bank account,
  without treating the transaction as a cash advance. (Cash
  advances generally trigger high interest rates and fees.)

When they find an offer, the arbitragers deposit the borrowed money into a
high-rate savings account, like those at ING Direct or EmigrantDirect.com,
and collect the interest. They make the required minimum payments until just
before the special low rate expires and then pay off the balance in full using
the money they stuck in the bank account.

To make much money, though, you have to borrow a lot. One woman
who discussed her activities with me made $1,700 in her first six months
while maintaining balances of $85,000 to $100,000 on her high-limit cards.

I'll be clear: this is a high-risk activity and not one I'd recommend for
most people. Missing even a single payment on a card can cause your rate to
soar and wipe out any benefit. Forget to pay the balance off in time, and the
same thing happens. Carrying big balances on your cards can also hurt your
credit scores.

And it simply won't work if you use the cards for other purchases (which
accrue at a higher rate) or aren't careful to read (and understand) every single
word of the balance transfer offers.

Those who do it and succeed must be extremely detail-oriented, have
great credit, and be willing to do the work involved to find the deals. If this
describes you, check out the forums at FatWallet.com for more details.

If You Pay Off Your Balance in Full Every Month

Here's where credit cards get fun.

Play them right, and you can get free trips, cash back, and other rewards.
But you have to find the right ones, understand how they work, and stay vig-
ilant to get the best deals.

Is this easy? Maybe not at first. But once you get the hang of it, you'll
need to invest relatively little time to make your cards pay off. If you combine
rewards cards with other rewards programs, you can really make money with
your spending.

Today's rewards cards have gotten so rich, in fact, that CardRatings.com's
Curtis Arnold says users should shoot for at least a 1.5 percent return on their

spending. Some rewards card users boost that return to 10 percent or more by taking advantage of various deals and programs.

Just one example: Discover Card typically offers a rebate of .25 percent to 1 percent, depending on how much you charge. But, in certain categories of spending that change every three months, Discover offers 5 percent rebates. Early in 2007, for instance, Discover had a three-month deal where travelers were offered 5 percent rebates on airline tickets, hotels, and rental cars charged to the card.

Let's say you booked a round-trip flight on your favorite airline from Philadelphia to Los Angeles, a ticket that cost you $500. In addition to the 4,800 frequent flyer miles you would earn for this trip—miles that are worth about 1.5 cents on average, or $72—you'd earn a Discover rebate of $25. If you used that rebate with one of the merchants that doubles Discover rewards, you could get a gift card worth $50. So with $500 of spending, you've earned rewards worth $122.

Not a big traveler? No problem. There are by one estimate over 40,000 different credit card rewards programs out there that offer everything from discounts on your next car purchase to extra payments on your mortgage.

Many people try to maximize their rewards by charging everything they can. (They're helped by the fact that many businesses, utilities, and other vendors now allow you to charge your bills.) Some even juggle a wallet-full of cards trying to make the most of their spending.

One young man who emailed me regularly used six cards that offered different rewards for various classes of spending:

- For gas, groceries, and drugstore purchases, he used his Chase Rewards Plus Visa, which offered 5 percent rebates on those categories.

- For books, movies, music, and restaurants, he used his Citi mtvU Visa, which offered 5 percent back on those categories.

- For airline tickets, he used his Citi Premier Pass, which gave him one point per dollar spent, plus one point for every three miles he flew.

- Two of his cards offered extra rewards on categories of spending that regularly changed. He used is Discover Card for purchases that qualified for the 5 percent rebate that quarter, while his RBS Custom Cash MasterCard gave him 3 percent cash back on one purchase category that changed each month.

- Any purchase that didn't fall into these categories was charged to his Orchard Bank MasterCard, which gave him 2 percent rebates.

He kept track of his rewards (and the cards' due dates) using Yodlee.com. In two years of relatively light spending, he'd earned $700 in rebates and two free domestic round-trip tickets.

My hat's off to him, but keeping track of that many cards is the opposite of "easy money." You'll get most of the reward and a fraction of the hassle picking one or two good reward cards that fit with your spending.

Still, you need to understand the downsides of rewards cards, including these:

- **Constantly changing deals**—The richer the rebate, the less likely it is to last. Some cards, like Discover, are explicit about the fact that their deals change, while others ratchet back offers more quietly. Citi Platinum Dividends Rewards reduced its best deal, 5 percent back on purchases made at groceries, gas stations, and pharmacies, to 2 percent without much fanfare.

- **Caps, tiers, and other limits**—Many cards cap the amount of reward you can earn in a single year, which makes them a poor choice for heavy spenders. Others penalize light users by requiring a certain level of spending before the top rebate rate kicks in. Discover Card requires $3,000 of annual spending before you get its top rebate, but purchases at many discount stores including Costco, Sam's Club, and Wal-Mart earn just .25 percent.

- **Credit score damage**—You risk dinging your score by 5 points, and sometimes more, every time you apply for a new credit card account. Opening a bunch of cards in a short period just compounds the damage. You can hurt your scores even more by maxing out your cards as you run after rewards, even if you pay the balances in full every month. For the sake of your scores, you should try to keep your charges to 30 per-cent or less of your limits (ask your issuer to raise your limits if necessary) and apply for no more than one or two cards a year. Don't apply at all if you're in the market for major bor-rowing such as a mortgage or an auto loan. Wait until your loan closes before seeking more credit.

- **High interest rates**—If you carry a balance, you'll want to get a card with the lowest interest rate you can find, and that won't be a rewards card—those typically carry rates in the high teens.

How to Find the Best Card(s)

Given the huge universe of cards, the constantly changing deals, and the varying pattern of people's spending, there's no one card that's right for everybody. Here are the different general types of cards, though, to help you narrow the field:

- **Airline frequent flyer cards**—These are credit cards affiliated with various airlines that give you (typically) a mile for every dollar you spend. It sounds great, except that airlines are making it tougher and tougher to redeem the miles you earn, which means these cards are usually not a good fit for the casual traveler. If, on the other hand, you're one of the airline's elite frequent flyers—someone who flies 25,000 or more miles with the carrier—these cards can be a great fit. You're at the front of the line when the airline hands out upgrades and free flights, so you can put your card miles to good use. You also might like an airline-affiliated card if you're trying to pile up miles for free international flights, particularly if you want to travel business or first class. Miles redeemed this way can be worth 8 cents each or more—lots better than the 1.6 cents that the average frequent flyer mile is worth.

- **Travel rewards cards**—Instead of earning a mile, you typically earn a point for every dollar spent. These tend to be more flexible than airline cards; you can typically use your rewards to book flights on any airline, for example, without worrying about blackout dates. You'll also have plenty of other options for spending your rewards, from free hotel nights and merchandise to gift cards. The problem with rewards cards is that the exchange rate may be 1 cent per point or less, and you generally can't get upgrades.

- **Cash-back cards**—I recently polled several credit card experts about what they carry in their own wallets, and the

majority favored cash-back cards for their rewards and simplicity. One card, in fact, was repeatedly mentioned:
American Express Blue Cash, which (as of this writing)
offered up to 5 percent rebates on purchases made at super-
markets, gas stations, and drugstores and up to 1.5 percent on
all other purchases. (The top rebate rate kicks in after the first
$6,500 in annual spending, but there's no limit on the amount
you can earn, both of which make this a card for heavy charg-
ers.) Unlike some other cards, you don't have to ask for Amex
Blue Cash rebates—they're automatically credited to your
account. Because Amex isn't accepted everywhere, the card
experts also carried a Visa or MasterCard with a cash-back
program. You generally want to avoid cash-back cards that
charge annual fees—the best ones don't.

• **Savings rewards cards**—These cards limit the actual *kind* of
rebate you can get, but they typically reward you with a
higher-than-average rebate *amount*. And instead of giving you
cash or rewards directly, these cards either deposit the booty
into a savings or investment account or offer some kind of
discount on a big purchase. For example, the Fidelity
Investment Rewards Visa deposits 1.5 percent of all your purchases into your Fidelity investment account (which you need
to have, obviously, to take advantage of the program). Citi has
cards that earn you discounts on vehicles as well as payments
toward your mortgage, among many, many others. The GM
card also earns you rebates of up to 3 percent on vehicle purchases. If these rewards coincide with your goals, they can be
a great choice.

After you've decided on the general category of card you want, you'll still
have to sort through the different card offers. You can check out the recommendations at CardRatings.com, drop in on the finance thread at
FatWallet.com, and use the interactive calculator at CreditCardTuneUp.com
to help narrow the choices. The calculator allows you to input how much you
expect to charge each month overall, as well as how much you spend in different categories (restaurants, home improvement, utilities, and so on), and
then recommends various cards or combinations of cards. You can see how
much more you can earn by adding one, two, or three cards to your mix and
decide for yourself if the extra reward is worth the extra hassle.

Even if you want to keep things simple, though, you probably should have at least two cards. It's smart to have a backup in case your main card is lost or stolen and you have to wait for a replacement.

When you sign up for online access to your rewards card accounts, you'll also want to sign up for its email newsletter. This can alert you to special deals, such as increased rewards for certain purchases.

Finally, check your rewards versus spending ratio at least once a year. Add up how much you spent on cards and the value of any rewards you redeemed during the year to see if you're at or above the 1.5 percent mark. (Rewards, points, and miles earned but not redeemed don't count because the issuer can always change the value by making them harder or easier to cash in.) Then check to see if there are any better rewards programs out there than what you're using. You don't have to switch every year—in fact, for the sake of simplicity and your credit scores, you probably shouldn't—but an annual checkup will ensure you're still at least getting a fair deal compared to what else is available.

Your Checklist

Here's your list of things to do from this chapter.

If you carry a balance

- ☑ Stop using your cards.

- ☑ Make a budget to free up money to pay off your balances.

- ☑ Negotiate with your card issuers for lower rates.

- ☑ Consider lower-rate balance transfer offers.

- ☑ If you can't pay off your balances within five years, consult with a legitimate credit counselor and a bankruptcy attorney.

If you don't carry a balance

- ☑ Review any rewards cards you have and determine the rate of return on your spending.

- ☑ Use CardRatings.com, Bankrate.com and CreditCardTuneUp.com to evaluate your options.

- ☑ If you decide to switch cards, apply for no more than one or two cards a year.

- ☑ Check your rewards versus spending ratio annually.

- ☑ Sign up for the email newsletter associated with your rewards programs, so you are aware of special offers.

The No-Sweat Guide
to Retirement
(and other) Investing

The tips, tricks, suggestions, and techniques I've given you so far have, I hope, made your life easier and saved you some money.

The advice I'm about to give, though, is *really* going to simplify your life and save you a fortune. Here it is.

Don't try to beat the market.

By "market," I mean the stock market in all its permutations: the New York Stock Exchange, the NASDAQ, and all the international exchanges. These are places where investors buy and sell stocks, which are little pieces of ownership in companies.

Most of us need to invest in stocks if we ever hope to retire. That's because of all the investments in the world, only stocks have consistently delivered high-enough returns to not only beat inflation but to build nest eggs capable of supporting people in their retirement years.

Average Annual Returns 1926–2006

Investment	Return
Large-company stocks	10.4%
Small-company stocks	12.7%
Bonds	5.4%
Cash	3.7%
Inflation	3.0%

Source: Ibbotson Associates. The following benchmarks were used: For large-company stocks, the Standard & Poor's 500; for small-company stocks, the bottom 20 percent of companies by market cap on the NYSE and companies of similar size on the NASDAQ and AMEX; for bonds, long-term government bonds; for cash, the 30-day Treasury bill; for inflation, the Consumer Price Index.

Inflation is constantly eroding the buying power of our money. Every year, a dollar is worth a little bit less. After 20 years, a dollar's value has been cut in half even with a seemingly low inflation rate of 3 percent. So if you stuffed $100,000 in your mattress 20 years ago and pulled it out to spend now, it would be worth about $54,300 in today's dollars.

Even if you put the cash into a money market account or short-term Treasury bonds, you would barely keep up with inflation. If you had to pay taxes on the interest—which you would if the investments weren't in a tax-deferred account like a retirement fund—you'd inevitably fall behind.

If you wanted to take a little more risk and get a little higher return, you might turn to bonds. Bonds are basically IOUs that governments and corporations write to investors. You're essentially lending money to these entities in return for interest.

But it's awfully hard to build a fortune, or even a decent retirement fund, on bonds alone. Let's say you wanted to create a $1 million next egg in 30 years. If you invested in long-term bonds and got the average return over the past 80 years, you'd need to set aside $1,095 a month.

If you invested in large-company stocks instead and got the average annual return, you'd need to set aside just $406 a month.

But stocks, clearly, have their dangers. Their values can plunge or even disappear if the company that issued the shares goes bankrupt. (Think Enron or WorldCom.) It's much harder to imagine a Treasury bond becoming worthless, considering it's backed by the full faith and credit of the U.S. government.

The swoop-and-swoon nature of the stock market is why *you should never invest money in the stock market that you're going to need within 10 years.* Bonds, bank certificates of deposit, and money market accounts are much more appropriate vehicles for shorter-term goals. But if you're investing for a goal that's 10 or more years out, such as retirement or a young child's college fund, you almost certainly need to put a big chunk of your money into stocks.

How to Manage Risk

The smart way to manage the risks of the stock market is through *diversification*. That's a fancy word for a simple concept: don't put all your eggs in one basket. Investing in a variety of different companies, as well as cushioning stock investments with bonds and cash, will help you take advantage of the market's superior returns while spreading your risk around to manageable levels.

There are three basic ways to build a diversified stock portfolio:

- With individual stocks

- With mutual funds

- With exchange-traded funds

Now, it's pretty tough for a small investor to build a truly diversified portfolio stock by stock. One financial planner I respect estimated that an investor needs at least $250,000 to build an adequately diversified portfolio of individual stocks; another, equally good planner put the amount closer to $1 million.

And here's another rub: when you have individual stocks, you need to watch them like a hawk. Since a company's fortunes can change on a dime, you have to carefully research your choices, monitor the companies and industries for changes, and be prepared to buy or sell on a moment's notice if circumstances change.

There are people who love the risks and challenges that such investing poses. The rest of us have lives to lead. Personally, I have a husband, a child, a household, and a business to run. I have friends and relatives I need to keep up with, an exercise routine I try to squeeze in, volunteer work I want to do. I've got a towering pile of work-related reading, and my roses are looking a little neglected. I'm not exactly sure where I'd fit in another full-time job, which is what individual stock investing essentially requires. Fortunately, I don't need to try.

Mutual funds offer pretty much instant diversification. Each one invests in hundreds or even thousands of different companies. They offer professional managers who either actively buy and sell stocks (an approach known as active management) or who ensure that a fund replicates some kind of market benchmark like the Standard & Poor's 500 or the Wilshire 5000. (This approach is known as *passive management*, which I prefer for reasons I'll discuss later.)

The third approach, using exchange-traded funds or ETFs, has some advantages and a few drawbacks. Like index funds, many ETFs try to replicate a market benchmark. The most popular ETFs include SPDRS, or Spiders, which track the Standard & Poor's 500 index of large companies; Powershares QQQ, which tracks the technology-heavy NASDAQ 100; and iShares Russell 2000, which tracks an index of small-company stocks.

Unlike funds, which are traded just once a day, ETFs can be bought and sold throughout the day, which makes them popular among active traders who want to make a bet on which way the markets will blow. But the very low annual expenses of many ETFs—some have annual costs of less than one-tenth of one percent—also make them popular with thrifty buy-and-hold investors.

For example, Vanguard Total Stock Market Index, an index mutual fund, has a very low annual expense ratio of .19 percent, or $19 for every $10,000 invested. That's great compared to the $100 or so the typical actively-managed mutual fund would charge for the same investment. But Vanguard's Total Stock Market ETF charges just 0.07 percent, or $7 for every $10,000 invested.

ETFs also tend to be quite tax efficient, generating a much lower tax bill than the typical mutual fund.

Not all ETFs are dirt cheap, of course. The more narrowly focused an ETF is, the higher the expenses tend to be. ETFs that focus on single industries, rather than on replicating a larger benchmark, tend to have particularly high costs.The biggest problem with ETFs for individual investors, though, is that you have to pay brokerage commissions to buy them. Even if you use a discount brokerage, the commissions offset much of the low-cost advantage unless you're investing a large sum all at once. So consider using ETFs if you're investing a big windfall, like an inheritance, or rolling over a big 401(k) balance into an IRA. ETFs typically are not a good fit if you're making a series of smaller investments over time, which is the usual model for ongoing 401(k) and IRA investing.

If you want to learn more about ETFs, start with the ETF center at Morningstar.com.

WHAT ABOUT REAL ESTATE?

The dot-com boom and bust at the turn of the 21st Century was followed by another big boom: the sharp run-up in residential real estate values in many parts of the country. With values rising 20 percent or more in some cities, many people thought they'd found a sure-fire way to wealth. Who needs the stock market when your home is worth a small fortune?

Booms can't last forever, though, and in 2006 prices in many areas hit plateaus or even fell. Nationally, the median price of a single-family home started dropping in the fourth quarter of that year—a trend that continued into 2007 as a subprime mortgage meltdown and credit crisis has rocked the financial and real estate markets.

Historically, residential real estate has appreciated at a little over 6 percent a year. But rising prices are only part of the story. Appreciation figures don't capture the vast amounts of money people spend financing, insuring, maintaining, repairing, and improving their homes, or the property taxes they pay. In some desirable and high-priced areas, like San Francisco, homeowners can still come out ahead. But in many others, homeownership may be a wash or actually a losing proposition.

That doesn't mean you shouldn't become a homeowner or that real estate shouldn't be part of your investment portfolio. What it means is that you shouldn't expect your home to be a substitute for a well-diversified retirement fund.

Why Beating the Market Is So Tough

There's another concept that you need to understand about investing. It's essentially a zero-sum game. For every buyer, there is a seller; for every gainer, there is a loser. The gains and losses of investors, combined, are what make up a market's returns. All together, we are the market average.

Now, you can't invest without costs. If you buy and sell individual stocks or "load" mutual funds, you have to pay commissions—either big commissions to a full-service brokerage firm or smaller commissions to a discount brokerage. If you invest with professional managers or mutual funds, you pay annual expenses and other management fees.

Once you've deducted those costs, the "average" return suddenly becomes below average. To put it another way: all of us, together, can only eke out a return that's less than the market average because of the costs we pay to invest.

And the extent to which we pay those costs is generally the extent to which we fail to keep up with market averages. The higher the costs, the further behind we fall. Study after study has shown that the higher the costs and the more that investors trade, the worse they do.

The key to wringing good returns out of the market is to keep costs down, and that means pursuing a low-cost, passive approach to investing.

Now, there's no shortage of people who want to convince you of the opposite. They hawk books, seminars, Web sites and newsletters that promise to teach you the secret of scoring above-average returns. If they make their living through commissions—as stockbrokers and many other financial advisors do—their job is to persuade you that you shouldn't "settle" for the market average, or a bit below it, but instead shoot for the stars.

This counsel certainly makes money for those pushing it. It's unlikely, however, that such advice will pay off for you.

There are a few investors who, over long periods, do manage to beat the odds and the markets. That's one of the reasons that billionaire Warren Buffett is so famous in the investing world. Although his calls aren't always right, they've been right often enough to build him (and many of his investors) a fortune.

Even though Buffetts exist in the world, it's impossible to figure out in advance who they'll be. You can make a bet that you'll be one, or you can hitch your wagon to a stock-picker or mutual fund manager who's trying to beat the odds by actively buying and selling. But chances are you'll be wrong.

If you want to explore these concepts further, there are two books you can read: Burton Malkiel's classic, *A Random Walk Down Wall Street* and Vanguard Mutual Fund founder John Bogle's *The Little Book of Common Sense Investing*.

Be aware that even seemingly small differences in investment costs can make a big difference over time. Let's suppose you're choosing between a mutual fund with annual expenses of .75 percent—which is well under the 1.25 percent average—and one whose expenses are just .25 percent a year.

If you invest $500 a month for the next 30 years and both funds average 8 percent annual returns, you'll have $67,476 more if you'd picked the lower-cost fund.

The Three Keys to Successful Investing

The diversified, passive, low-cost approach is not just a better way to invest. It's a heck of a lot easier. Your choices become a lot clearer and you have to make far fewer decisions, both upfront and along the way, than when you're trying to pull off a more active approach.

Here, then, are the three keys to being a successful investor.

Use Low-Cost, Broad-Market Index Funds Wherever Possible

As noted earlier, index funds mimic market benchmarks like the Standard & Poor's 500 Index, which represents 500 large, mostly U.S.-based companies.

But if you want to harness the true power of the stock market, you won't settle for just large companies. You want midsize and smaller companies as well. If you can, seek out index funds that track the broader U.S. market, such as Vanguard's Total Stock Market Index, Schwab's Total Stock Market Index, or T. Rowe Price's Total Equity Index.

These funds don't really buy every company on the market. Vanguard's version, for example, invests in 1,200 to 1,300 of the companies represented on the MSCI U.S. Broad Market Index, which in turn represents 99.5 percent of the total value of all the companies regularly traded on U.S. exchanges. Schwab's fund, meanwhile, seeks to replicate the Wilshire 5000 Composite Index, which represents all the companies on mainstream exchanges. Either fund, though, will give you the exposure you need to a variety of shares.

You'll likely want some exposure to foreign companies, since many foreign economies are growing at a faster pace than ours. Some good international index funds include Fidelity Spartan International Fund, Schwab Total International Index, and Vanguard Total International Stock Index Fund.

Now, you may not have immediate access to the funds I've recommended or others like them. Most 401(k)s, for example, have a limited number of investment options, and some don't include index funds at all, or they only include an S&P 500 fund. If that's the case, don't worry; I have advice later in this chapter about cobbling together a winning portfolio.

By the way, I should mention that index funds have another advantage important to many investors: they're quite tax-efficient. Because their managers aren't constantly buying and selling stocks, index funds don't generate the big capital gains tax bills that their more actively managed peers create. If you're investing outside a tax-deferred account, index funds can keep your tab to Uncle Sam pretty low.

Include Bonds and Cash in the Mix

For a while during the dot-com boom of the late 1990s, it was fashionable among many investors to pretend that bonds and cash were for weenies.

The notion was that *true* long-term investors—and that was supposed to include all young people and most everyone else under 70—had plenty of time to ride out any stock market downturns.

This was an easy philosophy to have when stock market gains regularly exceeded 20 percent a year. As the 2000–2002 bear market started chewing into people's portfolios, though, this point of view started seeming a lot less smart.

In fact, I heard from a lot of folks who saw their nest eggs fall by 50 percent or more and who had to postpone retirements or go back to work to try to make up for their losses. Others lost their heads entirely and sold their entire stock portfolios in a panic—thus missing the recovery that followed.

Meanwhile, those of us who kept a dash of bonds and cash in our pokey little portfolios did all right. My family's investments took a slight dip and then treaded water for a while before going on to post regular gains.

It's not that bonds and cash can't lose value. As you read, inflation and taxes can eat into their returns. The actual value of bonds can also rise and fall depending on prevailing interest rates and the prospects of the entities that issued them. But the rises and falls tend to be less dramatic than for stocks, and they're usually on a different time table. In other words, when stocks are down, bonds may be up. And cash investments like money market accounts and short-term Treasury bills are almost always "up;" your returns might drop to 1 percent or 2 percent, but they'll still be in positive territory.

So bonds and cash form an important cushion for your overall portfolio. They can keep you in the game, in other words, when you're tempted to run for the exits.

Add a Dab of Real Estate

Real estate tends to gain and lose value on a different cycle than stocks, so investing in a real estate investment trust (REIT) can reduce your risk. REITs typically invest in commercial properties, large apartment complexes, shopping centers, and hotels across the entire country. So you're also insulated from regional swings in value, such as the real estate recessions that hit Boston, Texas, and Alaska in the 1980s and Southern California in the 1990s.

Exactly how you should divide your investments depends on a number of factors—so many, in fact, that good financial planners can spend hours going over the details of your financial life and your tolerance for various kinds of risk before compiling a recommended portfolio.

You won't go too far wrong, though, if you follow a classic balanced portfolio, which looks like this:

- Broad-market U.S. stock index fund: 40 percent

- Broad-market foreign stock index fund: 20 percent

- Broad-market bond index fund: 20 percent

- Real estate investment trust: 10 percent

- Cash (money market or Treasury bills): 10 percent

If you're young or a bit of a gambler, you might ratchet up the portion of your portfolio that's in stocks. If you're approaching retirement age, you might want to reduce your stock exposure—although many planners recommend that you not go below 50 percent, especially if you plan to spend 20 years or more in retirement.

If you're investing a large lump sum all at once, you can get similar diversification with exchange-traded funds, such as the following:

- Vanguard Total Stock Market ETF (ticker symbol VTI): 40 percent

- Vanguard FTSE All-World ex-USA Index Fund (VEU): 20 percent

- iShares Lehman Aggregate Bond (AGG): 20 percent

- Vanguard REIT Index ETF (VNQ): 10 percent

- Cash: 10 percent

Rebalance Annually, but Otherwise Leave Your Investments Alone

The last key to a winning portfolio is rebalancing.

When you rebalance a portfolio, you bring it back to its original or target "asset allocation." Asset allocation is essentially how your investments are deployed among various types of investments, such as U.S. stocks, foreign stocks, bonds, and cash. (You can take it even further by breaking down each type into different categories, such as large, midsize, and small company stocks, or by different investment styles, such as growth, value, and blend.)

You might start out with 40 percent of your total portfolio invested in a U.S. broad stock market index fund. If U.S. stocks go on a tear, as they did in the late 1990s, the value of that index fund will swell and could become a much larger portion of your portfolio, say 60 percent or more. If the U.S. market plunges (as it did in 2000–2002), you'll sustain a lot more pain than you would have if you had rebalanced your portfolio to the original 40 percent target.

There are a few challenges involved with rebalancing.

- **It's hard to sell "winners" and buy "losers"**—That's basically what you're doing: reducing the portion of your portfolio that's done well recently and deploying that money in stuff that's done poorly (or not as well as the winning stuff). But you've got to do it if you want to manage your risk.

- **It may involve costs**—There may be commissions involved in buying and selling your investments. If the investments you're selling are held outside tax-deferred accounts—in a taxable brokerage account rather than an IRA or 401(k)—you would owe taxes on any profits you've made. If you're trying to keep taxes down, consider redirecting new contributions into your "non-winning" investments instead until you've returned to your target asset allocation.

- **It's easy to procrastinate—or overdo it**—Rebalancing involves effort (plus a bit of courage), so it's easy to put off. At the other end of the scale are folks who, once started, can't leave well enough alone. They're constantly tweaking their portfolios after every market rise and fall. Instead of being passive investors, they've switched to overactive mode, focusing way too much time and energy on their investments for little (if any) additional return.

Moderation is the key. An annual rebalancing should be all you need to set your portfolio right and continuing sailing.

If you're daunted by the task, though, you do have other options.

Why Life-Cycle and Target Maturity Funds May Be the Answer

Mutual fund companies and 401(k) plan providers have, somewhat belatedly, realized that most people don't want to become mini-investment gurus. They don't want to have to sort through a bewildering array of investment choices, figure out how much to invest in each, and then constantly tweak their portfolios.

Even the easy approach—using a mix of index funds and rebalancing once a year—is more effort than many people want to make.

Enter life-cycle and target maturity funds, which do the work for you.

Life-cycle funds allow you to choose a fixed investment mix. A life-cycle fund targeted to growth, for example, might invest 75–80 percent of its investors' funds in stocks and put the rest in bonds. A moderate or balanced fund might opt for a 60 percent/40 percent mix, while a conservative fund will typically have most of its money in bonds and cash and the rest in stocks. As time goes on, the fund manager rebalances the portfolio to remain true to the fund's stated investment mix.

These aren't quite "buy and forget" funds, however. If you're in your 20s and 30s, you probably want a "growth" lifestyle fund, but as you near retirement, you'll want to reduce your risk. That means selling your growth life-cycle fund and buying a moderate or conservative version instead. But that's still a lot less effort than rebalancing a portfolio every year, and it's a heck of a lot less effort than trying to actively manage your investments.

If you want even less work, however, target maturity funds may be for you. You pick a single fund that does all the asset allocation and rebalancing for you, potentially for the rest of your working life. Each fund has a year in which it's scheduled to "mature"; you pick the one that's close to the date you plan to retire. If you plan to leave work in 2042, for example, you pick the fund that matures in 2040. Vanguard, Fidelity, T. Rowe Price, Schwab, and many other financial services companies offer target maturity funds.

A few things to keep in mind:

- **These funds are meant to stand alone**—You miss the point if you buy a target or life-cycle fund *plus* a bunch of other funds in the same portfolio. In most cases, this should be one-stop shopping.

- **Costs can vary**—Unfortunately, not all lifestyle and target maturity funds use index investments. Instead of employing a passive approach, they may invest in actively managed funds, which tend to increase their operating expenses (and waste money in my book).

If the lifestyle options in your 401(k) charge 1% or more, and you have access to index funds that cost less, it may make sense to skip the convenience of a lifestyle fund and put together your own, lower-cost collection of index funds.

Target funds with the same maturity dates can have different asset allocations. Vanguard Group funds, for example, tend to be a bit more conservative, while T. Rowe Price target maturity funds can start off with an aggressive mix.

You can compensate for these differences fairly easily, though. If you want to invest more aggressively with Vanguard target-date funds, just pick the one that's dated ten years past your planned retirement date. If you plan to retire in 2030, for example, pick Vanguard Retirement Fund 2040. If you want a somewhat more conservative approach than what you're offered in a target fund, pick a date that's five to ten years earlier than you plan to retire.

In any case, before you invest, it pays to do a little research. A subscription to Morningstar.com will give you access to detailed reports about the investment mix, performance, and expenses of the funds you're considering.

VARIABLE ANNUITIES: A NON-STARTER

I could write a whole chapter—no, a whole *book* about why you almost certainly don't want one of these in your retirement portfolio. Variable annuities are basically mutual fund-like investments wrapped in an insurance policy, and they're a really, really expensive way to invest. They're costly not just because of the fees that insurance companies charge (which reduce your returns) but because of the awful tax treatment you get when you withdraw the money. And if you plan on giving any of the leftover money to your heirs—fuhgeddaboudit. Annuities don't get the all-important "step up" in tax basis that other investments get. That means you've essentially increased the tax burden for your heirs.

Variable annuities offer tax-deferral while you're working, but you already have that in your 401(k), IRA, and other retirement accounts. Variable annuities also come with a much-touted death benefit, which guarantees that your heirs will get back whatever money you invested, even if your investments have dropped in the meantime. The chances of your dying while the market's down are pretty slim, though, and you'd typically be better off just buying term life insurance if you're worried about your heirs. Many annuities now have "living benefits," which purport to lock in your gains during your lifetime, but you'll pay through the nose for those.

If you really want to educate yourself on the topic, you'll find a ton of information on the Web and in books devoted to retirement. If you still decide you must have one, at least do yourself the favor of buying the lowest-cost version you can directly from a provider like Vanguard, Fidelity, or T. Rowe Price.

But I'll leave you with this observation: people who make commissions from selling variable annuities love them. People who know about financial planning, though, know there are almost always better alternatives.

Which Account Do I Use?

401(k). 403(b). Roth IRA. Roth 401(k). Traditional IRA. 457s.

These are just some of the options you have for saving for retirement. Some—like 401(k)s or 403(b)s workplace plans, 457 deferred compensation plans, and many traditional individual retirement accounts (IRAs)—offer tax breaks up front. Your contributions are deductible, and your withdrawals in retirement are taxed at regular income tax rates.

Neither Roth IRAs nor Roth 401(k)s offer deductions for contributions, but withdrawals in retirement are tax free.

Each account has its own limits and restrictions. With 401(k)s and 403(b)s, you can typically contribute up to $15,000 a year in 2007 and $15,500 in 2008. People 50 and over to contribute an additional $5,000. If your company offers both a regular 401(k) and a Roth 401(k), the annual limit covers both. You can commit the full $15,000 to either account or split it between the accounts, but you can't contribute $15,000 to the regular 401(k) and then another $15,000 to the Roth 401(k).

Contributions limits for IRAs are much lower. IRAs also come with other restrictions.

How Much Can I Contribute to an IRA or Roth IRA?

Year	IRA Contribution Limit	50 and Over
2006–2007	$4,000	$5,000
2008 and after	$5,000	$6,000

If your income is high, your ability to contribute to a Roth IRA may be restricted (see below). And contributions to a traditional IRA aren't deductible if you're covered by a workplace plan like a 401(k) *and* your income exceeds certain limits. In 2007, the ability to deduct a regular IRA contribution when you have a workplace plan began to phase out for single people with incomes over $50,000 and married couples with incomes over $80,000.

Who's eligible to contribute to a Roth IRA? Anyone with earned income can contribute to a Roth IRA unless their income exceeds certain limits. In the phase-range, contributions are pro-rated.

Am I Allowed to Contribute to a Roth IRA?

Tax Filing Status	Income Phase-Out Range (2007)
Married filing jointly or Head of household	$156,000 to $166,000
Single	$99,000 to $114,000

So how do you decide?

The traditional rule of thumb has been that if you expect to be in a lower tax bracket in retirement, choose accounts that give you the up-front deductions. If you expect to be in the same or a higher tax bracket, choose options that offer you the tax break at the end—Roth IRAs, Roth 401(k)s.

Most people, at least historically, wind up in a lower tax bracket in retirement. But you may not—particularly, if you're young or building up a substantial net worth. Also, the U.S. government has considerable deficits, while Social Security and Medicare systems are headed for financial crises. The probable fix for these problems: higher taxes in the future.

Besides, Roth IRAs and Roth 401(k)s offer an additional and potentially valuable benefit: you don't have to withdraw the money. While other retirement accounts require you to start taking distributions after age 70½, Roth IRAs have no such rules. (You can roll a Roth 401(k) directly into a Roth IRA, which means you can avoid distribution requirements with that money as well.) So if you don't need the money, you can leave it to your heirs.

Given all the uncertainties, you might want to hedge your bets: put some of your retirement contributions into accounts that give you an immediate tax break and some into accounts that promise the tax break in retirement.

Here's one example of how this might work:

1. If you have a 401(k) or other workplace retirement plan with
    a company match, contribute enough to get the full match.

2. Then fund a Roth IRA, if you're eligible.

3. Can you still contribute more? If you have a Roth 401(k)
    option at work, you can put it there, or you can split the
    money between the Roth 401(k) and the regular 401(k).

However you decide to contribute, do yourself a favor and keep your hands off the money until you need it in retirement.

Avoid the temptation to borrow or withdraw from your retirement money. If you leave a job and can't leave your 401(k) account where it is, arrange to have it rolled over into an IRA or into your new employer's plan. Keep your tax-deferred money working for you; don't derail your retirement plans by raiding the kitty prematurely.

Coordinating Your Approach

Of course, many people already have more than one retirement or investment fund. You might have a couple 401(k)s from previous jobs as well as an IRA or two and a few taxable brokerage accounts. If you're part of a couple, you may have a whole raft of 401(k)s, 403(b)s, IRAs, Roth IRAs, and other retirement plans.

To simplify your life and reduce costs, you should first consolidate your accounts as much as possible. You may be able to transfer those old 401(k) accounts into your current employer's plan, for example; if not, you can roll them into an IRA. You can't, however, put another person's retirement funds into your account, or vice versa; and you can't combine IRAs with Roth IRAs (at least not without paying a bunch of taxes and following the IRS' rules on Roth conversions; see a tax pro for details).

Once you've consolidated, you can start coordinating your strategy.

Let's start with the example of a couple. If you're committed to staying together and all your accounts have the same goal—such as retirement—you should view your investments as a whole to make sure you're not taking too much or too little risk.

There are a few ways to accomplish this. The easiest way is to use only target maturity funds. Another approach is to figure out your desired asset allocation and replicate it in each one of your (perhaps many) accounts.

The problem is that you might not have access to target maturity funds in every account, or you may not want to use the ones you have. Also your spouse might have a really good, cheap U.S. broad-market index fund in his or her 401(k) while you have only actively managed stock options but a pretty great bond fund. If that's the case, you might want to put 40 percent of your *combined* retirement contributions into her great index fund and 30 percent into your awesome bond fund, even if that means you wind up allocating all or nearly all of an account's contributions to a single fund.

Here's an example. Let's say you make $50,000 annually while your spouse makes $25,000, but you both contribute 10 percent to your respective 401(k)s, or a total of $7,500 annually ($5,000 from you, $2,500 from your spouse). You want to use the asset allocation suggested earlier and put 40 percent of your total contributions into a broad-market U.S. stock fund. If your spouse's broad-market option is superior, your spouse would wind up contributing his or her whole $2,500 contribution to that fund. You would put an additional $500 (10 percent of your total contributions) into your own

401(k)'s broad-market choice, and you'd deploy the rest of your contributions into the great bond fund ($2,250, or 45 percent of your contributions), the okay foreign fund ($1,500, or 30 percent), and the cash option ($750, or 15 percent).

Single people trying to coordinate workplace and individual retirement accounts should do essentially the same thing. Figure out your overall asset allocation strategy and put your individual accounts to best use.

Your 401(k) may have pretty good stock choices but no foreign funds or a high-cost bond fund. You can use your IRA or Roth IRA to balance out those weaknesses. Just make sure your investments, as a whole, hew to the asset allocation you want and rebalance once a year.

Getting Help

You should be able to put together a good, easy-to-maintain investment portfolio on your own. But some people really want some extra hand-holding. Fortunately, there are places you can go to get objective, personalized advice.

- **Through your job**—Employers are increasingly willing to hook up their workers with advisory firms that can offer personalized retirement plans and investment advice. Some use actual human beings, while others use software programs to create recommended portfolios. The cost is typically free to you.

- **From an independent advisor**—In my opinion, fee-only financial planners are the way to go. These advisors are compensated only by the fees you pay them and not by commissions or other payments based on the products they sell. You can get referrals from the National Association of Personal Financial Advisors (www.napfa.org) or the Garrett Planning Network (www.garrettplanningnetwork.com). The cost varies widely and can range from a couple hundred bucks for a portfolio review to a couple thousand for a full-fledged financial plan. You'll find more information on selecting a financial planner in Chapter 8, "When You Need Help."

- **From your mutual fund company or brokerage**—I advise steering clear of commission-based planners and brokers, but some mutual fund companies and discount brokerages— including Vanguard, Fidelity, Schwab, and others—offer personalized portfolio reviews for reasonable fees (typically a few hundred dollars).

- **From the Web**—There used to be several Web-based applications that would review your goals, risk tolerance, and 401(k) options and then spit out customized portfolios. Many of them have disappeared or deal only with corporate clients, but FinancialEngines.com still takes on individuals in addition to its larger business of advising company 401(k) plans. The cost is about $40 a quarter. FinancialEngines.com uses sophisticated Monte Carlo simulations to figure your probabilities of success with various portfolios and gives advice about other accounts, such as IRAs, in addition to reviewing your workplace retirement plans.

How Much Should I Save for Retirement?

We've dealt with *how* to invest for retirement goals. Now let's deal with the equally important question of how *much* we should invest.

The short answer: nobody knows for sure.

Projections of how much we need to salt away for our later years are, at best, educated guesses. So many of the factors that go into the calculations can't be predicted with certainty, including but not limited to these:

- How long you'll live

- How your investments will perform

- How much inflation you'll face

- What will happen with Social Security

- When you'll retire (you may be bumped out of the job market by accident or illness—or ultimately decide you never want to quit)

- What your living expenses will be

- What medical and long-term care costs you'll face

- Whether your long-lost Uncle Rich will leave you a fortune or blow it on an exotic dancer

That doesn't mean you get to throw up your hands in frustration and walk away. You know you're going to need *something* to sustain you in old age— and probably a big pile of something. You don't want to eke out your last years regretting that you didn't put enough away.

It's also not as if we're totally in the dark. History has given us a pretty good blueprint for what we can probably expect as far as inflation (3 percent or so) and investment returns (8 percent is a good, if slightly conservative, average annual estimated return for a balanced portfolio). Your health, lifestyle, and genes can offer clues into how long you might live. (MSN Money has a Life Expectancy Calculator that might prove illuminating.) Your current spending gives *some* idea of how much you may need in retirement, and your needs will become clearer as you age.

Social Security remains a big question mark. The trustees who run the program say it will start paying out more benefits than it receives in taxes in a few years, and it will be technically broke by 2041, so clearly something needs to change.

Because the program was designed as a safety net for the elderly, I believe it is unlikely that Social Security benefits will be cut significantly for the lowest-income workers. I'm not so sure about medium-wage earners, and I think high-wage folks could take a real haircut.

If you're a low-wage earner or close to retirement, you can probably count on receiving the amounts promised in the benefits estimate you get from Social Security annually in the mail. The younger you are or the more you make, however, the more you may want to discount those numbers. Figure that you'll receive half or less of what you're currently promised.

There are many retirement calculators on the Web and two good ones packaged in the Quicken and Money personal finance software. But to get you started, you can use the Ballpark E$timate® that follows.

Ballpark E$timate®

Planning for retirement is not a one-size-fits-all exercise. The purpose of Ballpark is simply to give you a basic idea of the savings you'll need to make today for when you plan to retire.

If you are married, you and your spouse should each fill out your own Ballpark E$timate® worksheet taking your marital status into account when entering your Social Security benefit in number 2 below.

1. **How much annual income will you want in retirement?**
   (Figure at least 70% of your current annual gross income just
   to maintain your current standard of living; however, you may
   want to enter a larger number. See the tips below.)

   $ _____

   Tips to help you select a goal:

   - **70% to 80%**—You will need to pay for the basics in retire-
     ment, but you won't have to pay many medical expenses as
     your employer pays the Medicare Part B and D premium
     and provides employer-paid retiree health insurance. You're
     planning for a comfortable retirement without much travel.
     You are older and/or in your prime earning years.

   - **80% to 90%**—You will need to pay your Medicare Part B
     and D premiums and pay for insurance to cover medical
     costs above Medicare, which on average covers about 55%.
     You plan to take some small trips, and you know that you
     will need to continue saving some money.

   - **100% to 120%**—You will need to cover all Medicare and
     other health care costs. You are very young and/or your
     prime earning years are ahead of you. You would like a
     retirement lifestyle that is more than comfortable. You need
     to save for the possibility of long-term care.

2. **Subtract the income you expect to receive annually from:**

   - **Social Security**—If you make under $25,000, enter $8,000;
     between $25,000 - $40,000, enter $12,000; over $40,000,
     enter $14,500 (For married couples, the lower earning
     spouse should enter either their own benefit based on their
     income or 50% of the higher earning spouse's benefit,
     whichever is higher.)—$ _____

   - **Traditional Employer Pension**—a plan that pays a set dol-
     lar amount for life, where the dollar amount depends on
     salary and years of service (in today's dollars)
     —$ _____

   - **Part-time income**—$ _____

- **Other (reverse annuity mortgage payments, earnings on assets, etc.)—$ _____**

    This is how much you need to make up for each retirement year: =$ _____

    Now you want a Ballpark E$timate of how much money you'll need in the bank the day you retire. For the record, we assume you'll realize a constant real rate of return of 3% after inflation and you'll begin to receive income from Social Security at age 65.

3. **To determine the amount you'll need to save, multiply the amount you need to make up by the following factor.**

Age you expect to retire: Choose your factor based on life expectancy (at age 65):

	Male, 82	Female, 86	Male, 89	Female, 92	Male, 94	Female, 97
55	18.79	20.53	21.71	22.79	23.46	24.40
60	16.31	18.32	19.68	20.93	21.71	22.79
65	13.45	15.77	17.35	18.79	19.68	20.93
70	10.15	12.83	14.65	16.31	17.35	18.79

4. If you expect to retire before age 65, multiply your Social Security benefit from line 2 by the factor below.

    If you expect to retire at 55, multiply your SS benefit by 8.8. If you expect to retire at 60, multiply it by 4.7.

    +$ _____

5. Multiply your savings to date by the factor below (include money accumulated in a 401(k), IRA, or similar retirement plan). If you plan to retire in 10 years, your factor is 1.3.

    15 years 1.6
    20 years 1.8
    25 years 2.1
    30 years 2.4
    35 years 2.8
    40 years 3.3
    −$ _____

Total additional savings needed at retirement: =$ _____

> Don't panic. We devised another formula to show you how much to save each year to reach your goal amount. This factors in compounding. That's where your money not only makes interest, your interest starts making interest as well, creating a snowball effect.

6.   To determine the ANNUAL amount you'll need to save, multiply the TOTAL amount by the factor below.

If you want to retire in 10 years, your factor is .085.

15 years .052
20 years .036
25 years .027
30 years .020
35 years .016
40 years .013
=$_____

The Ballpark E$timate® is designed to provide a rough estimate of what you will need to save annually to fund a comfortable retirement. It provides an approximation of projected Social Security benefits and utilizes only one of many possible rates of return on your savings. Ballpark reflects today's dollars and does not account for inflation; therefore, you should recalculate your savings needs on a regular basis and as your salary and circumstances change. You will not want to stop with the Ballpark E$timate®; it is only a first step in the retirement planning process. You will need to do further analysis, either yourself using a more detailed worksheet or computer software, or with the assistance of a financial professional.

What if you can't possibly save as much as the Ballpark E$timate® or other calculators say you should? Don't despair. Here are some easy strategies to consider:

*   **Just start somewhere**—Sign up for your company's 401(k) or other defined contribution plan, even if you're only able to contribute 1%. (And trust me, *anyone* can contribute 1%.) If you don't have a plan at work, set up an automatic transfer of 1% of your pay so that it's electronically moved from your checking account to an IRA or a Roth IRA. (Look for a

brokerage or bank that has few fees and low minimum contribution requirements. ING Direct, for example, allows you to
open an IRA or Roth IRA with a contribution of just $25
a month.)

- **Commit your raises**—Boss just raised your pay by 3%?
  Boost your 401(k) or IRA contributions by at least half
  (1.5%, in this case). Several folks who post on MSN's "Your
  Money" message board have been doing this for years and
  say it's a remarkably painless way to save. You still get a little
  increase in your checks, but you've also put more money to
  work for your retirement. (You can put even more to work, of
  course, by putting your entire raise into your retirement kitty.)

- **Celebrate your savings**—As soon as you pay off a loan or
  reduce some other expense, redeploy the freed-up money to
  your retirement accounts. Don't wait or waffle—if you procrastinate, you're likely to find some other (much less important) use for the money.

- **Deploy your windfalls**—A portion of any chunk of money
  that falls into your lap (such as an inheritance, an insurance
  settlement, or a tax refund) should be tucked into your retirement accounts. If you have an IRA, you can deposit the cash
  directly. If you have a 401(k) or other workplace plan, you
  can temporarily increase your contribution rate and tap your
  windfall to make up for the reduction in your paychecks.

One final thought on how much to save: if you're young and trying to decide
how much to put away, err on the side of "too much." Seriously. In my 20s, I
regularly saved 20 percent or more of my income, and I'm glad I did. Those
savings became the foundation of the comfortable net worth we have now,
and I really didn't feel like I sacrificed back then. I still took plenty of trips,
pursued hobbies, and had a great time with friends. I just did it on the money
I had left over after I funded my 401(k) and IRA.

Getting in the habit of saving big bucks early also gives you the priceless
gift of flexibility. You can cut back when you're older and face more
expenses, take a few years off work to raise a child without endangering your
financial plans, and have a lot more say not only in when you retire but how
you'll live when you do.

Though it may be hard to believe now, someday you will be old, and
you'll thank your younger self.

As You Approach Retirement

You'd be smart, as you get closer to retirement, to set up a meeting with an objective, qualified financial planner to review your portfolio and discuss how you're going to tap your funds in retirement. Such a consultation is a good idea when you're within five years of retirement; it's absolutely essential before you give notice to your workplace that you're going to retire.

Preretirement planning is complicated enough, and the penalties for mistakes so severe, that it's well worth paying for a professional review of your situation.

Take out too little money, for example, and you could earn the IRS's wrath (along with pretty hefty penalties). Take out too much or at the wrong time, and you could wind up depleting your funds too quickly.

The amount you can safely withdraw from a portfolio is, in fact, remarkably small. Leading financial planners put the safe withdrawal rate at around 3 percent or 4 percent of your portfolio in the first year of retirement, with the dollar amount adjusted each year afterward by inflation. If your portfolio is worth $500,000, for example, you could take out $20,000 the first year; if inflation runs around 3 percent, your next year's withdrawal would be limited to $20,600.

Now, some planners argue that you can safely withdraw somewhat more in retirement, particularly if you stay heavily invested in stocks or if you anticipate your spending declining in later retirement (as it often does). Personally, I'd prefer to err on the side of caution and risk having too much money in retirement over running out of money too early.

If you want to see how much money you can safely withdraw from a portfolio, look for the retirement income calculator at the T. Rowe Price's Web site (www.troweprice.com/ric). The calculator allows you to adjust for your portfolio's asset allocation and your probability of success (which basically means the chance that you won't run out of money).

While you're discussing options with your financial planner, ask about the possibility of buying an immediate annuity, particularly if you don't have a traditional pension and Social Security payments won't cover your basic expenses.

Wait a minute, you might be saying. Didn't I just say annuities were an awful investment?

The annuities sold to most people, *variable* annuities, are often a bad fit. But immediate annuities are a different animal.

With an immediate annuity, you hand over a lump sum of cash to an insurance company that promises in return to send you a stream of checks, usually for the rest of your life. Typically, you get a set amount of money in each check, in effect creating your own traditional pension. You can also build in inflation protection, if you'd like.

A 65-year-old woman, for example, might purchase an immediate annuity from Vanguard for $100,000. In return, she would get monthly payments of $643 for the rest of her life. If she wanted inflation protection, her initial payment would be lower—$455—but her checks over time would be adjusted to reflect the rising cost of living.

Annuities can be complicated, and you'll want to discuss your options with a qualified, objective professional. You particularly want to make sure that you're buying from a financially strong insurer and that you're getting the most for your money—in other words, that an excessive amount of your cash isn't going toward fees or other costs.

But an immediate annuity can provide definite peace of mind and financial security in a world where both are increasingly rare.

Your Checklist

Here's your list of things to do from this chapter.

☑ Determine how much you need to save for retirement using the Ballpark E$timate® or another retirement calculator.

☑ Figure out how you want to divide your contributions among your available tax-deferred retirement options.

☑ Set up (or revise) automatic transfers into the appropriate accounts.

☑ Review your current portfolios' performance, costs, and asset allocation using Morningstar.com.

☑ Consider alternatives, including index, balanced, life-cycle, and target maturity funds.

☑ Implement any necessary changes.

☑ Rebalance annually.

☑ Consult a fee-only planner as you near retirement.

5

The Easy Way to Save
for College

Does this anxiety dream sound familiar?

You're back at college, roaming the campus. Suddenly you discover that you're late for a final exam. That's bad, but your next realization is worse: the final is for a class you forgot to attend.

For a lot of parents, the complexities of saving for college evoke the same emotions: confusion, panic, and a seasick certainty that their mistakes will doom them (or their offspring).

Here's what parents have to deal with

- Education costs that continue to spiral at double the rate of inflation

- A raft of different savings vehicles—custodial accounts, Coverdells, 529 college savings plans, prepaid tuition programs—with different rules, restrictions, tax treatments, and effects on financial aid

- Complex federal and private aid formulas that can zap you for saving the "wrong" way

Can you navigate this maze? Of course. But let's cover the basics of what you need to know, such as the following:

- **Your own retirement has to come first**—Yes, you want to give your children a good start in life, but not if that means having to move in with them when you're 70. Make sure you're saving adequately for your own retirement before contributing to a college fund.

- **If you *can* save for college, you probably should**—Many parents fret that they'll be "punished" for saving by getting smaller financial aid packages. In reality, most college savings vehicles are treated pretty favorably by federal financial aid formulas. The exception: custodial accounts, also known as Uniform Transfer to Minors Act (UTMA) or Uniform Gifts to Minors Act (UGMA). If you've got money in one of these, try to spend it down—on tutoring, academic camps, computers— before the child is a junior in high school. The higher your income, the less likely you are to receive aid anyway—the assumption being that you *should* have been saving for college, even if you didn't.

- **Don't expect a free ride**—Full scholarships are awfully rare, and it's much harder these days to be considered an "independent" student for financial aid purposes than it was a generation ago, so you shouldn't count on either option erasing your responsibility to save.

- **Starting early is good, but anything you save will help**—Put $250 a month into a college account from the time your child is born, and you should have around $120,000 by the time she's 18, assuming 8 percent average annual returns. Wait just five years to start, and you'll need to cough up $440 a month to get a similar result. But that doesn't mean you should despair if your kid's in high school and you still haven't started, since any money you do manage to save will cut down on the debt she will have to take on to pay for college.

- **A good calculator can get you on track**—The "World's Simplest College Calculator" at SavingForCollege.com, a site run by CPA Joseph Hurley, is a great way to get started. You can fiddle with the type of education you want (public or private), the investment returns you expect, and the percentage of the total tab you want to cover.

I used the calculator to come up with these estimates of how much you would need to set aside each month based on your child's age to fund:

- 100 percent of a private college education

- 100 percent of a public college education

- 50 percent of a public college education

As you can see, trying to save for a private school education is expensive, even if you start early. A more affordable goal might be to shoot for covering the cost of a public education (or half the cost of a public school, if that's all you manage).

Monthly Savings Required to Fund College Education

Age	100% of Private*	100% of Public**	50% of Public
Newborn	$644	$279	$139
5	$808	$350	$175
10	$1,110	$481	$241
15	$1,898	$823	$411

Based on current average cost of $30,000, including tuition and room and board

**Based on current average cost of $13,000, including tuition and room and board*

Figures assume college costs rise at an average annual rate of 6 percent while investments grow at an average annual rate of 8 percent.

- **Be smart about debt**—If you can't save enough to pay the whole bill, loans can come to the rescue—*but they probably should be the student's loans,* not yours. After all, your child is the one who will benefit from the increased income a college education generally brings. And you don't need to be taking on more debt so close to retirement. Just make sure that your child doesn't borrow more, in total, than he expects to make in annual salary the first year out of school. If that amount of debt, plus your savings, isn't enough to pay for college, you need to look for less expensive education options—a state school rather than a private one, for example, or an in-state school instead of out-of-state, or two years in a junior college before transferring to State U.

  This advice really rubs some parents, and their progeny, the wrong way. Some feel they have a God-given right to the best university education possible, regardless of the cost.

  But the consequences of this "price tag blindness" can be severe. Overspending on a child's education can delay parents' retirement for years or leave them financially vulnerable to setbacks, like disability or illness, that cut their working years short.

Overdosing on student loans can have equally horrific consequences. I've heard from way too many young graduates who
are facing decades of student loan payments. The amount they
owe is often enough to preclude saving adequately for their
own retirements or buying a home. Some can't even afford
the minimum payments on the massive debts they've
incurred.

And that's a big problem, since this is debt you can't escape.
Student loan debt typically can't be discharged in bankruptcy
court, and student lenders today have powerfully effective
ways of collecting their due, including wage garnishment.
This debt can quite literally follow you to the grave. In one
famous case, collectors garnished the Social Security check of
an elderly, disabled man for unpaid student loans; the U.S.
Supreme Court upheld the collector's right to take 15 percent
of the man's $874 monthly benefit check.

So treat student loan debt with respect and make sure you can
actually afford the education you're buying.

Why 529 College Savings Plans Rock

Now that you've got the fundamentals, you're ready for the good news. One
method of saving for college has emerged head-and-shoulders above the rest:
529 college savings plans.

These state-administered programs allow you to invest money that can be
used tax-free for college expenses. (The tax-free aspect of the plans was set
to expire in 2010, but Congress has made it permanent.) What's more, 29
states and the District of Columbia offer their residents tax breaks for contributing to the plans. Some states also offer extra tax credits to lower-income
families to encourage them to save in the plans.

Respected financial services firms, including Vanguard, T. Rowe Price,
TIAA-CREF, and Fidelity, operate the plans under contract with the states.
Although some plans were initially criticized for high expenses and poor performance, public pressure has led to lower fees and increased investment
options in many states.

The benefits of 529 college savings plans are significant and numerous.

- **The accounts are given favorable treatment in federal
  financial aid formulas**—Typically, 529 college savings plans

are considered the parent's asset, which means that no more than 5.6 percent of the total account would be counted "against" the student each year. Distributions from the account to pay for college expenses aren't counted at all. Contrast that to custodial accounts, including UTMAs and UGMAs accounts. These accounts are considered the student's asset, and the family is expected to contribute 35 percent of the total account's value each year.

- **The contributor—not the child—controls the account—** Again, this is quite different from custodial accounts, where any money not used for education gets turned over to the child (typically at age 21). With college savings plans, there's no requirement that the child ever get the money if he doesn't go to college or doesn't need the funds. The account can be transferred to another beneficiary, such as one of the child's relatives. The contributor can also use the money for his own education or simply withdraw it and pay income taxes (plus a 10 percent federal penalty) on any gains.

- **You can start small—**You don't have to shell out big bucks to start. At California's ScholarShare, for example, you can start with an initial investment of $50 and monthly contributions of just $15, and there's no annual fee.

- **There are great no-brainer investment options—**The typical 529 plan offers a number of different investment options, but the best one for most parents involves the least effort: the age-weighted portfolio. You hand over the money, and professional money managers deploy your contributions in a mix of stocks, bonds, and cash based on the age of your child. As your child gets older and college nears, the manager gradually dials back the risk so that you don't risk getting wiped out by a market downturn right when the first tuition bill is due.

- **There are few limits—**Anyone can contribute to a 529, regardless of income, and the total amount that can be contributed is high: typically $250,000 or more. That's in sharp contrast to Coverdells (formerly Education Savings Accounts), which impose income limits on contributors and cap annual contributions at $2,000 (an amount that's scheduled to drop to $500 in 2010 and thereafter).

- **There are astounding estate-tax benefits**—This matters
  only if you, your parents, or a particularly generous auntie has
  big bucks and is trying to reduce future estate taxes. But if
  that's the case, you should know about the extraordinary benefits of contributing to a 529 college savings plan.

  Usually, you can give no more than a certain amount to
  another person without having to file a gift tax return. In
  2007, this "gift tax exemption" amount was $12,000. But
  when the contribution is made to a 529 college savings plan,
  you can give five years' worth of exemptions at once—or
  $60,000. If both Grandma and Grandpa wanted to give to
  your little Susie, the total amount they could give without
  having to file a gift tax return would be $120,000.

  That alone is pretty awesome, but for the contributor, it gets
  even better. Although the gift is considered "completed" for
  estate tax purposes—in other words, if Grandma and Grandpa
  die tomorrow, the money wouldn't be counted in their
  estates—*they still have control over the money.* So they can
  switch beneficiaries *or even take the money back* if it turns
  out they need it.

  Hopefully, of course, they won't renege on their gift, but the
  ability to reclaim the funds if necessary can go a long way
  toward convincing otherwise conservative folks to make such
  a gift.

Picking the Right College Savings Plan

As you can see, the decision to invest in a 529 college savings plan is a pretty
easy one to make. The next decision is more complicated. Which plan should
you choose?

After all, every state has a 529 plan, and many states have several. Each
of the plans may have a dozen or more investment options. Clearly, that's a
lot to wade through. Here's how to winnow down your choices.

- **Start at home**—Most states give residents a tax deduction for
  529 plan contributions. As of this writing, three states—
  Kansas, Maine, and Pennsylvania—give you a state income tax
  deduction even if you invest in another state's plan. Other
  states are considering similar extensions, but most that have tax

deductions require you to use the in-state plan. The tax break can be a powerful incentive to stick with your own state's plan, but even the best break may not compensate for a poorly performing, high-cost plan. Check SavingForCollege.com to get the lowdown on your state plan's fees and options.

- **Go cheap**—If the annual costs are over .75 percent to 1 percent a year, or if you have to use a broker to invest, look elsewhere. High annual expenses just eat into your returns (and can easily offset any tax deduction you got for your contributions). And if you use the plan's age-weighted option, as I recommend, it makes no sense to lose a big chunk of your contributions to broker commissions. The only reason you might want to pay a broker is if you're getting good stock-picking or asset allocation advice, which you're clearly not if you use the plan's no-brainer option.

- **When in doubt, choose Vanguard**—Vanguard is pretty much the low-cost leader when it comes to mutual funds and 529 college savings plans. The company runs several states' plans, and its funds are included as investment options in others. The company's Web site, www.Vanguard.com, offers links to those plans.

Prepaid Tuition Plans

So far, when referring to 529s, I've been discussing the kind of plans that work something like 401(k)s: you contribute money, and what you get at the end depends on your account's investment performance, minus any fees. There are no guarantees you'll have enough at the end to pay for college.

But there's another kind of 529 plan, and that's the prepaid version. In essence, you're allowed to buy blocks of tuition in advance, locking in the price and protecting yourself against future tuition inflation. If tuition rises after you've purchased the blocks, it doesn't matter, since a semester purchased now will still buy a semester's worth of education 10 or 15 or 20 years from now.

Most of the state plans cover tuition at any in-state public college or university. A plan for private schools, the Independent 529 Plan, allows parents and others to prepay for tuition at any of the more than 250 participating schools, including Amherst, Smith and Wellesley colleges, and Stanford, Tulane, Notre Dame, and Princeton universities.

Until recently, these plans weren't a good option for many families because they got terrible treatment in financial aid calculations. Congress corrected that problem in 2005, though, and now federal financial aid formulas give prepaid tuition and college savings plans the same favorable treatment.

But prepaid plans still aren't for everyone because of the following:

- **Limited selection**—Not every state offers them, and those that do typically require either the contributor or the beneficiary (the child) to be a resident. (There's also an Independent 529 Plan—more on that later.)

- **Relatively low "yield"**—Because of the way prepaid plans are structured, they're probably best suited for conservative investors. If you're willing to take even moderate amounts of risk, you'll likely wind up with more money by doing your own investing in a college savings plan. Also you pay a premium over current tuition costs to lock in the blocks of prepaid schooling, and it takes a while for tuition inflation to offset that premium. That makes prepaid plans a better idea for families with young children than for those whose kids are already in high school.

- **No guarantees**—Even though these plans are advertised as "guaranteed" ways to save, there's nothing guaranteeing their continued existence. If states don't price the tuition blocks properly or their investment returns falter, the plans can be shuttered. Several states, including Colorado, Kentucky, Ohio, Texas, and West Virginia, have stopped accepting new enrollees due to financial problems, and New Mexico actually closed its plan and refunded participants' contributions.

- **Restricted use**—At the state-run plans, the blocks typically must be used at one of the state's public colleges and universities. If the student goes out of state or to a private school, the plan figures out how much tuition your investment would buy, on average, at an in-state school and gives you that refund in cash, minus any administrative fees.

  If you buy through the Independent 529 plan and your student isn't accepted by one of the participating schools, or he decides to go elsewhere, the plan refunds an amount equal to your original investment plus an annual gain of no more than 2 percent.

These drawbacks are what make college savings plans a better option for most families. But if you've got young kids, are reasonably certain they'll attend a covered school, and really want the peace of mind these plans can bring, you should at least investigate the prepaid option.

Your High School Game Plan

This chapter dealt with saving for college. Once your child starts high school, you're going to want additional help in strategizing the best approach to higher education. You'll want advice on evaluating colleges; pointers on financial aid; and up-to-date information on the latest tax breaks.

Fortunately, there are some great guidebooks out there. Two of my favorites are *Paying for College Without Going Broke* by Princeton Review and *FastWeb College Gold: The Step-by-Step Guide to Paying for College* by Mark Kantrowitz and Doug Hardy. Scoop up the latest editions of these books and educate yourself on the possibilities.

Kantrowitz' Web site, www.FinAid.org, is another invaluable resource. Among other nifty tools, it has a financial aid calculator that can give you an idea of how much schools will expect you to contribute. Families with young children should use the calculator as a wake-up call to get them saving more; families with older kids can use it as a way to help them plan for the expenses ahead.

What to Do If You're Starting Late

If your kids are already in high school and you haven't started saving yet, don't panic. Every dollar you manage to save is likely to spare them a dollar or more of debt. Here are some things to consider.

- **A prepaid plan isn't your best choice**—Tuition costs probably won't rise enough to offset the extra premium that these plans charge. (See the earlier section.)

- **A regular college savings plan may or may not be the right choice**—You should be investing conservatively if you'll be using the money within four years, which means lower returns and, as a result, less of a tax break. Some experts believe the restrictions on using 529 college savings plan money outweigh the benefit of any break you'd get when you're starting so late, but I think it's still a good choice if you're in the 25 percent federal tax bracket or above.

- **Hit up your folks**—If your parents are well-off and so inclined, they can help your children and their own estate-tax situation considerably by contributing to their college savings plans (see earlier section) or paying college costs directly. (The gift-tax limits don't apply when grandparents pay education bills directly.)

- **Consider your alternatives**—You (or your progeny) may have had your heart set on four years at an ivy-covered private institution. But many public universities deliver as good or better educations for less money. Another option: your kid goes to a high-quality community college for two years and then transfers to a four-year school. You'll save a bundle, and your kid will still get a diploma from the better-recognized school.

Your Checklist

Here's your list of things to do from this chapter.

- ☑ Determine if you can save for college and, if so, how much.

- ☑ Evaluate your college savings options.

- ☑ Arrange for automatic transfers to the plan of your choice.

- ☑ As college approaches, review guidebooks that can help you enhance your financial aid prospects and arrange an affordable education for your kids.

6

Insurance: Protecting What You Have—And Will Have

Years of writing about insurance and answering readers' questions have convinced me that many people think about insurance the wrong way.

Too many view insurance not as a safety net but as a gamble or some kind of investment plan. They want their premiums to "pay off" or at least cover expenses that they don't think they should have to pay. These folks feel their premium dollars have been wasted if they don't see a check from their insurance company.

This backward thinking leads people to buy the wrong insurance, spend too much, make too many claims, leave themselves wide open to unforeseen catastrophe, and in general cost themselves small fortunes.

The better way to think of insurance is as the ultimate safety net. You want to use insurance *to cover the catastrophic expenses that you couldn't easily cover on your own.*

Viewed that way, insurance becomes something you have but (generally) hope you'll never need, since a payout means you or your family has experienced a major disaster.

If you do need it, though, you want to make sure it's there in sufficient quantities to protect you from losing everything you have and everything you're ever going to have (to paraphrase Clint Eastwood's character in *Unforgiven*).

Here's what you need to know.

Auto Insurance

You might think it would be hard to be both underinsured and overinsured on the same policy, but it's not. In fact, it's pretty common with auto insurance.

To understand how, you have to know something about this coverage, which consists of three basic components:

- **Liability coverage**, which pays for the damage you do to other vehicles, property, and people in an accident

- **Collision coverage**, which pays for damage to your car when you cause an accident

- **Comprehensive coverage**, which pays for damage or loss that occurs from something other than a crash (such as a thief stealing it or a tree falling on top of it)

Many people, in a misguided attempt to keep their premiums low, opt for the lowest possible liability coverage. Unless you're dead broke and on disability, though, that's almost certainly a mistake. If you're sued after causing an accident, you may wind up having to sell just about everything you own and fork over big chunks of your future income to cover the bill. Instead of opting for the minimum, get at least 100/300/50 coverage, which pays $100,000 to each injured person up to $300,000 per accident, plus $50,000 for property damage. If your net worth is over $300,000, you should buy even more coverage—perhaps equal to one or two times your net worth. (If your net worth is really above average, you may need to get additional coverage known as an umbrella or personal liability policy. More on that later.)

At the same time people underinsure themselves on liability, they may overinsure by choosing a low deductible or hanging on to collision and comprehensive coverage long after it makes sense.

Collision and comprehensive coverage typically make up 25 percent to 50 percent or so of your total premium. But the check your insurer would give you after an accident or theft shrinks pretty rapidly over time. At a certain point, the trade-off between premiums and insurance proceeds tips to the point where it no longer makes much sense to keep the coverage.

Now, you may not have much choice. If you leased the car or borrowed money to buy it, you may be required by your contract or loan agreement to keep this coverage until you turn in the car or pay off the loan.

But if you have a choice, you should at least consider whether to drop the coverage.

To see how much you might get from your insurer, use Edmunds.com or Kelley Blue Book (www.kkb.com) to estimate the current value of your car if you were to sell it yourself. (This figure is usually somewhere between the car's trade-in value and the price a dealer would charge.) This is approximately the amount your insurer would pay if you had comp and collision and your car were totaled or stolen.

Now look at your last premium statement. *If your annual premium for comprehensive and collision coverage is more than 10 percent of the value of the car, it's time to drop the coverage.*

As always, there are exceptions. If your finances are in such a bad way that you would be sunk without the insurance payment, paltry as it may be, then you may decide to hold on to the coverage a bit longer. For most people, though, the cost isn't worth the payoff.

Speaking of unneeded coverage, you want to take a look at what else you might be paying for unnecessarily. You probably need uninsured/underinsured coverage if it's offered in your state, but you may not need medical payments coverage if you have good health insurance. Rental car and towing coverage is often unnecessary, as well.

In addition to boosting deductibles and dropping unneeded coverage, you can reduce your auto premiums if you

- **Use public transportation or carpool**—If you dramatically reduce the miles you drive, your premium may decline dramatically as well, since so much is based on the number of miles you drive.

- **Get all the breaks you deserve**—Many insurers offer discounts for good drivers; good students; people who have taken defensive driving courses; households that cover more than one car or that insure their home as well as their cars; even certain professions, like engineers or teachers. Ask for a list of discounts your insurer offers and take any that are coming to you.

- **Maintain good credit**—Most states allow insurers to use credit or credit scoring formulas to determine your premiums. That might not seem fair to you, but insurers and independent researchers have detected a strong correlation between bad credit and the propensity to file claims. Paying your bills on time, paying down your debts, and applying for new credit sparingly can pay off in lower premiums.

- **Take a defensive driving course**—Even if your insurer doesn't give you a premium break for taking such classes,

you'll emerge a better and more careful driver. That will
reduce the odds you'll cause an accident that could send your
premiums soaring.

- **Minimize distractions**—Most people believe they're above-
  average drivers, which is, of course, statistically impossible.
  What's scarier, though, is the number of people who seem to
  think they can drive safely while talking on the phone, applying makeup, or performing any other distracting task. You
  don't have to spend much time on the road to see ample evidence of the folly of this thinking. Err on the side of caution
  and pull over if you need to use the phone. Do the same if
  you need to swap CDs, touch up your mascara, fiddle with
  your iPod, or discipline your kids. The tiny inconvenience is
  worth it, since a second's distraction can result in an accident
  that could change, or claim, lives.

- **Shop around for insurance**—I had high hopes early in the
  dot-com boom days that the Internet would make this process
  a breeze, but the reality has fallen far short of the hype. Even
  the best Internet quote sites represent just a small slice of the
  available insurers; filling out their forms can take a small
  eternity and require revealing lots of personal information.
  What's worse, many sites don't give you instant quotes. They
  "get you in touch" with insurance salespeople who call or
  email you (sometimes relentlessly).

But shopping for insurance is one of those annoying chores you just have to
do occasionally. Why? Because you can save hundreds, sometimes even thousands, of dollars by doing so.

There really is no consistency in how different insurance companies set
their premiums. If an insurer is trying to attract new business, either in general or in a certain area, it will slash its premiums. Its rivals may be trying to
get rid of customers in the same area and will jack premiums sky-high to do
so. Insurers manage their businesses very differently, and some embrace
risks—like young drivers or those with troubled credit—that others try their
best to avoid.

Here's just one example of how much rates can vary. According to the
California Department of Insurance, the amounts insurers charged for a Los
Angeles couple with a 17-year-old son in 2006–2007 ranged from a low of
$2,652 to a high of (get this) $15,824. Would you want to pay $13,000 a year
more than you had to? I thought not.

Every couple of years, you should make the effort to shop around to make sure you're getting the best rates. You can

- **Start with your state insurance department's Web site**— Many offer premium surveys that can give you an idea of which might be the low-price leaders for your area and situation.

- **Listen to the ads**—If a company is advertising heavily on local television and radio that it's offering the best rates, add them to your list of companies to call.

- **See what belonging gets you**—Membership in a group can win you discounts. AARP, for example, arranges insurance discounts for its members with selected companies. If you're current or former military (or the dependent of someone who is), check out USAA, which typically tops consumer surveys for service and price. Your union or employer may have arrangements with insurers to offer discounts, as well.

- **Try some Web sites**—Insure.com and Progressive, which offers its own quote as well as those from competing companies, are worth a try.

- **Consider seeking out an independent insurance agent**— These agents have relationships with more than one company and can shop your coverage around, saving you some time. Just don't expect agents to poll *every* insurer—they typically work with just a handful.

Renters Insurance

This section will be mercifully brief: if you're a renter, you need this coverage.

Your landlord's property insurance covers damage to the building—not to your possessions. It also doesn't cover you for liability. If a friend slips on your bathroom rug, cracks his head on the sink, and needs a lifetime of rehabilitative care, you're probably on the hook for that.

Fortunately, renters insurance is pretty cheap—generally just a few hundred bucks a year. Get quotes from a few different homeowners insurance companies, pick a policy, and sign up. There. You're done.

Condo Owners Insurance

Your condo association pays the bill for insuring most of the structure and outbuildings, but you're responsible buying liability protection and coverage for your condo's contents. Depending on how your condo agreement is written, you may also need to buy coverage for walls, appliances, or interior fixtures.

The easiest way to determine the coverage you need is to take a copy of your agreement to an insurance agent.

Homeowners Insurance

Like auto insurance, homeowners' policies can be divided into three broad components:

- Liability coverage

- Coverage for the structure and other buildings

- Coverage for your possessions

Liability coverage protects you if you're sued, such as if someone slips and falls on your walkway. As with auto insurance, you want liability coverage that's at least equal to your net worth, if not more—$300,000 is probably the minimum you should carry. (You may, by the way, have a hard time getting liability insurance, or wind up paying more for it, if you own something the insurer considers particularly dangerous, such as a trampoline or certain breeds of dog, such as a pit bull, Rottweiler, German Shepherd, husky or chow.)

Determining how much coverage you need for the house itself is a bit more problematic. What's important is not what you paid for your home, what you owe, or what it's worth now. What matters is how much it would cost to rebuild if it was destroyed today.

Unfortunately, most homeowners are underinsured. A survey by building cost experts Marshall & Swift/Boeckh LLC found that 58 percent of houses in 2006 didn't have sufficient coverage. On average, the policies would pay enough to cover only 80 percent of the average rebuilding costs.

How can this be? Some homeowners buy too little insurance to start, while others don't keep up with rising building costs or fail to consider the value of additions and improvements. Some are lulled into complacency by insurance agents who insist their coverage is adequate—when it's not. (Sometimes the agents don't realize their mistakes, and other times they're so eager to sell a policy that they may recommend too little insurance to keep the premiums down.)

Many people discover they're underinsured only after it's too late: when fires or other disasters level their homes. Some people erroneously believe that their insurers have to pay to rebuild their homes no matter what the cost, but today virtually all insurers limit their payout to 120 percent or so of the insured value of your home. So if you have $100,000 of coverage but your home costs $200,000 to rebuild, you'd have to come up with $80,000 out of pocket.

It's not unreasonable to ask your insurer to reevaluate your policy every year or so to make sure you have adequate coverage. Another easy solution: buttonhole a contractor who's building or remodeling in your neighborhood and get a square-foot estimate of how much a home in your area would cost to rebuild.

You also need to consider covering your home for catastrophic risks that aren't covered by the standard homeowners' policy. Flood damage, for example, is specifically excluded; if you want coverage, you need to buy it through a federal agency, the National Flood Insurance Program. (Your regular insurance agent should be able to get you a quote.) Likewise, earthquake and hurricane damage often aren't covered.

Many people fail to get catastrophic coverage, believing (incorrectly) that the government will bail them out in a disaster. In reality, the calamity that destroys your home may not be widespread enough to trigger government intervention, and even if it does, the amount of money you can get to rebuild is fairly small. Most government aid that's handed out comes in the form of loans that have to be paid back. So unless you're willing to take on even more home debt or to walk away from your house and your equity, you want to at least consider getting catastrophic coverage.

Now, there are some perils that aren't covered by any policy, like damage from war or nuclear disaster. There's not much you can do about those risks, but you do have power to prevent damage from long-term conditions like a slow water leak, dry rot, or termites—damage that typically isn't covered by homeowners policies either. (Insurers believe homeowners should detect and correct these problems in time to prevent major problems.)

Speaking of leaks, you need to know that a water-related claim can be particularly hazardous to make, even if it would clearly be covered under your policy. Insurers today are spooked about rising costs from water- and mold-related claims, and they aren't above effectively blacklisting people who make them. (Insurers share claims information in the Comprehensive Loss

Underwriting Exchange (CLUE) database, so other insurers may refuse coverage once your insurer has dropped you.) If you can possibly pay for this type of damage out of pocket, you should consider doing so.

You also need to consider your contents coverage. The amount you get may be related to the amount of insurance you have on the home itself: a policy that insures a house for $200,000 may provide 75 percent of that amount, or $150,000 of contents coverage. Or your insurer may use some other number or formula. Either way, your policy typically limits coverage on items like jewelry, silver, business equipment, and guns; to cover these possessions adequately, you may need to request (and pay for) extra coverage known as a rider.

You'll want to make sure your policy includes the words *replacement-cost coverage* for the contents of your home. Otherwise, you'll get a check for the *depreciated* value of your stuff—not what you paid for it or what it will cost to replace. The bedroom set that set you back $3,000 a few years ago might have been worth just a few hundred bucks by the time it was destroyed; a replacement-cost policy will pay you $3,000 so you can buy another one, while a so-called "actual cost value" policy will pay you the much lower sum.

Finally, you need to do a home inventory that catalogs everything you own, what you paid for it, and when. The easiest way to do this is by walking through your home with a video camera, taking time to record everything in every nook and cranny and discussing the relevant details. Keep the tape or film in a safe deposit box and consider making a duplicate to send to an out-of-state family member or friend, since the disaster that wipes out your home might also level your bank.

Here are some ideas for reducing your homeowners' insurance premiums.

- **Shop around**—As with auto insurance, homeowners' premiums vary widely by company. Use your state's database and the various Web quote services to check out the competition.

- **Raise your deductible**—You'll save money and reduce the temptation to make small, potentially premium-boosting claims.

- **Keep your home well maintained**—As noted earlier, preventable damage isn't covered. Catch and fix infestations, leaks, and other damage early.

- **Maintain good credit**—Again, as with auto insurance, a good credit history can result in lower premiums.

Umbrella Liability Policies

Umbrella or personal liability policies typically kick in when the liability coverage on your homeowners or auto policies has been exhausted. If someone successfully sues you for $1 million, for example, your homeowners or auto insurance would pay up to your liability limit, but you'd be responsible for the rest.

An umbrella policy sits over your existing coverage like, well, an umbrella, providing extra peace of mind for a relatively small price. (You can usually get a $1 million policy for about $300 a year.) You can typically buy an umbrella policy from your homeowners' insurance company, although some auto insurers and third-party insurers offer coverage as well.

If your net worth is already greater than the maximum liability coverage on your car and house policies, or if you might be a "lawsuit magnet"—a high earner or someone in the public eye—an umbrella policy is a good idea. Once again, shoot for an amount at least equal to your net worth and perhaps twice that much.

Some of my readers have asked about these liability rules of thumb. What prevents someone from suing you for a lot more than one or two times your net worth? Nothing, actually, but trial attorneys have told me that they typically will settle for the amount of liability coverage someone has, unless the person they're suing is really underinsured. Then the lawyers may take the trouble to go after the person's assets.

Health Insurance

For a few blissful years, our family enjoyed one of the last old-fashioned medical insurance plans.

We had our pick of doctors and hospitals. Co-pays were low. *And we didn't pay a dime in premiums.* The coverage was provided through my husband's union when he worked in the animation industry.

Such red-carpet coverage used to be the norm among U.S. employers, but that day has long since passed. The reason? It's prohibitively expensive.

In fact, when my husband switched back to teaching, we opted not to continue our gold-plated insurance plan. We would have had to pick up the entire cost ourselves, and that was well over $1,200 a month.

Instead, we opted for a high-deductible plan that requires us to pay the first $5,000 in annual medical bills out of pocket. In exchange, we pay premiums that aren't exactly low but are reasonable for today's health insurance climate.

In other words, we put our money where my mouth is: We have health insurance to protect against catastrophic expenses, and we pay the rest ourselves.

Obviously, what works well for us wouldn't work for others. If you have affordable health insurance options through your employer, for example, or your family needs a lot of medical care, it may make more financial sense to purchase an HMO (health maintenance organization) or PPO (preferred provider organization) plan. With each plan, you'll have to weigh the premiums you pay against the choice of providers and how much of your health care bill the plan covers. There's no easy way to predict what will be best—sorry. You have to examine the particulars of the plan.

If your employer offers health insurance, it may also offer flexible spending plans, which allow you to put aside pretax money to cover your deductibles and out-of-pocket medical expenses. These are a good deal for many families; if you're in the 25 percent federal tax bracket, for example, you save $250 for every $1,000 you put aside this way. The catch is that you have to use up the money before the end of the year (or March 15 of the next year at some companies).

If you don't have health insurance through an employer, though, or you're covering basically healthy people, a high-deductible plan (also known as catastrophic coverage) may be the answer.

In fact, the creation of Health Savings Accounts (HSAs) was designed to encourage more people to consider high-deductible polices. HSAs allow you (or you and your employer) to set aside money that can be invested (kind of like an IRA). If the money is used for medical expenses, it's tax free. The money can be allowed to grow for years or even decades and used to pay for retirement medical expenses, if that's what you want.

HSAs must be combined with a qualified high-deductible insurance plan, but you don't need to pick a deductible as high as ours is. Yours could be as low as $1,000.

If you'd like to know more about HSAs, visit www.HSAInsider.com for details.

Here's what you *don't* want to do if you can possibly avoid it.

- **Go bare**—It doesn't matter how healthy you are—you're one accident or illness away from catastrophe. If you lose your job, the COBRA law allows you to maintain your group coverage if you pick up the entire premium. That may be your best bet if you're in poor health; otherwise, consider buying an individual policy, high-deductible, or otherwise, directly from an insurer.

- **Opt for a low-limit plan**—Some companies provide "insurance" plans that have ridiculously low caps, like $10,000. These plans won't cover you for real catastrophes and should be avoided.

- **Ignore your state's resources**—Every U.S. state has an insurance plan for babies, children, and teens of low-income families. (That includes income of up to $34,100 a year for families of four in 2006.) Some extend coverage to parents as well. To find out if you might be eligible, visit InsureKidsNow.gov or call (877) KIDS NOW.

Disability Insurance

Linda suffered a number of financial trials in her life—divorce, then widowhood, then a long stretch as a single mother. The most potentially devastating blow, though, was her diagnosis of lupus, which forced her to quit work at 48.

Many people in her situation would be forced to eke out the rest of their existence on a small Social Security disability check—if they could qualify for that. But among the smart financial decisions Linda made early on was buying a long-term disability policy through her employer.

Today, her annual income is about $60,000—about 75 percent of what she made as a pipe designer for the oil and gas industry.

Here again, the right insurance became a much-needed safety net in a disaster.

You may know that your earning ability is your biggest asset. You may even know that you're far more likely to be disabled for at least three months during your working life than you are to die.

Yet if you're like most Americans, you don't have long-term disability insurance.

Many have workers' compensation for injuries sustained on the job—but not all disabling accidents happen at work, and disabling illness is rarely job related.

Social Security disability isn't an adequate substitute, either. You're only covered for total and long-term disability, not partial or short-term problems. Besides, it's pretty tough to get.

If your employer offers long-term disability, you should probably grab it, even though it has its disadvantages. Employer-provided coverage typically isn't portable, which means you can't take it to the next job, and it may not be as generous as you'd like. Many employer policies don't pay after the first two years unless you're totally disabled; if you can work a job—any job—even part-time, you could lose coverage.

On the other hand, employer-provided coverage is typically a lot less expensive—and easier to get—than buying a policy directly from a disability insurer. To be sure you're making the right decision, though, consider getting a few individual policy quotes from the major players, such as UnumProvident, Hartford, and MassMutual, so you can weigh your options. You might decide individual-policy coverage is worth the extra cost.

Or you might also consider an add-on policy to supplement your employer-provided plan. If your employer plan would replace only 50 percent to 60 percent of your income, an add-on policy might boost coverage to 75 percent.

Of course, buying an individual policy might be your only option if you can't get disability through your employer, your union, or a trade organization.

In any case, shopping for disability insurance isn't a do-it-yourself project. You'll need to work through an insurance agent, since disability insurance is complicated and you'll need guidance through the maze of policy provisions. You generally want to try to replace as much income as possible, with a minimum of 60 percent of your pay. You may have to agree to a longer waiting period—6 months instead of 90 days, for example—to make it more affordable. Finally, you should try for "own occupation," which will cover you even if you could do another, less desirable job.

Life Insurance

Successful life insurance agents are awfully good at what they do.

They break through people's squeamishness about death and get them to confront their own mortality. They simplify incredibly complicated policies into a few key selling points. And they typically have stirring tales of hand-delivering a big check to a widow or family who would have been financially devastated without the cash.

But they're also paid in a way that can encourage them to put their financial interests ahead of their customers. Thanks to the way commission structures are set up, life insurance agents often make more for an expensive policy that doesn't provide your family with adequate coverage than for a cheap policy that does.

Clearly, you have to be on guard.

Fortunately, though, there are really only two basic questions you need to answer when it comes to life insurance:

- Do I need it?

- If so, how much do I need?

For most people, the answers to those questions will dictate the coverage they buy and short-circuit the insurance industry's attempts to sell them expensive policies that may fall short.

The answer to the first question—Do I need it?—is yes if and only if *there are people who depend on you financially*. These folks typically include

- A spouse or partner who needs your income to pay the mortgage or basic living expenses

- Minor children

If you're single and childless, or your spouse would do fine without your income, you probably don't need life insurance. Any attempt to sell you on the bells and whistles of various life insurance plans is kind of pointless, since you have no need for the coverage itself and you have better things to do with your money.

The major exception: you're so rich that you worry about estate taxes. (Congress keeps changing the rules on estate taxes, but if your net worth is over $1 million, you probably should at least talk to an estate planning attorney about the potential tax liability.) If estate taxes may be an issue for you, you can afford to hire an objective third party to review any policy your agent is trying to sell you. (More on that later.)

If your spouse or partner does depend on you financially, or you have small children, you probably do need life insurance. That's true even if you're a stay-at-home parent, assuming your children are young enough that someone would need to be hired to look after them.

The next question—How much do I need?—is trickier to answer. In general, though, a married couple with small children should buy enough insurance to replace 8 to 10 times their annual income. If that doesn't describe your situation, or you want a more precise estimate, you can use the Life Insurance Needs Estimator at MSN:

http://moneycentral.msn.com/investor/calcs/n_life/main.asp

Once you decide how much you need, you're ready for the "term versus cash-value" discussion.

Term insurance is designed to cover you for a limited period (anywhere from a year to 30 years) and has no investment component. Cash-value policies include an investment component and may be referred to as "permanent" insurance because they can be designed to cover you for a lifetime.

Cash-value insurance sounds pretty nifty, but the niftiness comes at a pretty steep price. The premium for this coverage can be 10 times as expensive as for the same amount of term insurance.

That's why, for many people, term insurance is the answer. *Term coverage is the only way they can afford adequate protection for their families.*

Chances are pretty good you don't need "permanent" coverage anyway. Most people's need for life insurance ends when the mortgage is paid off, the kids are out of college, or they hit retirement age, whichever takes the longest. Although their families will still face funeral and burial costs at their death, those typically aren't the kind of catastrophic expenses that justify continuing life insurance.

(There are always exceptions to the rule, of course. As noted earlier, if you're wealthy and want insurance money to cover your estate taxes, you may decide to buy permanent coverage. Ditto if you have a disabled child who needs lifetime care. In these cases, a good cash-value policy can be a godsend.)

When buying term insurance, you should do the following:

- **Get a longer policy than you think you might need**—The cost for a 30-year policy usually isn't that much more than for a 20-year policy.

- **Get a guaranteed level-term policy**—You want a guarantee that your premiums will be the same every year you're covered. Otherwise, the premiums for your 20-year policy could jump sharply after the 1st, 5th, or 10th year.

- **Get a convertible policy**—You can't know what lies ahead, so it's good to have the option to convert your term coverage into a cash-value policy should you need it. (You may want to extend your policy after your health has gone south, for example; qualifying for coverage in that case could be extremely expensive without the conversion option. Or your fortunes may improve to the point where you want to give your heirs help paying estate taxes.) Some policies don't have a conversion option or offer it only for the first few years. You may need to pay more for a policy that has a conversion option that lasts as long as the policy does, but it may be worthwhile.

- **Shop around**—Life insurance rates vary enormously. At a minimum, get quotes from Term4Sale.com, Insure.com, and Ameritas.com. The first two offer quotes from a variety of insurers, while Ameritas is an insurer that sells directly to the public.

- **Think twice about buying additional coverage from your employer**—Many companies offer employees a certain base amount of life insurance (typically equal to their annual income, or $50,000) with the option of buying more. The problem with these policies is that you often can't take them with you should you leave your job. Some that are portable require you to convert first to expensive cash-value insurance, which may not be what you want. Also since they have to cover people of all ages and in all kinds of health, employer-provided policies are often more expensive than what you could purchase on your own. Explore your options, but if you're in good health, you'll probably want to buy your own policy from the company of your choice. Speaking of which...

- **Go with a highly rated company**—You want an insurer that is financially strong enough to be there when you need it. You can check insurance company ratings at the Web quote services or at A.M. Best, Fitch Ratings, or TheStreet.com Ratings.

If you're still confused or want more help in evaluating your options, talk to a fee-only (not "fee-based") financial planner. Fee-only planners are compensated solely by the fees you pay, not by commissions or fees from products that they sell. They can take an objective look at your situation and guide you to a qualified insurance professional, if that's what you need. You can get referrals from the National Association of Personal Financial Advisors (www.napfa.org or 888-FEE ONLY) or from the Garrett Planning Network (www.garrettplanningnetwork.com).

If you're trying to evaluate a cash-value policy—either one you already have or one you're thinking of buying—consider using the policy-evaluation service offered through the Consumer Federation of America.

For $60 to $75, insurance actuary and former insurance commissioner James Hunt will examine the policy and offer his analysis, which according to the CFA can help you

- Decide whether to buy a cash value policy or term insurance

- Decide among two or more cash value policies you are considering

- Decide whether your existing cash value policy is worth keeping

You can find more details at
    http://www.consumerfed.org/evaluate_insurance_policy.cfm

Finally, if you already have coverage, consider whether you should "refinance" it.

Prices for term life insurance dropped steeply through the 1990s and have continued to fall, albeit not quite as sharply, since then. What that means is that you may be able to get a cheaper policy now than a few years ago, even though you're older.

If that's the case, make sure your new, replacement policy is in place before you cancel the old one.

Your Checklist

Here's your list of things to do from this chapter.

Auto insurance

- ☑ Review your liability limits and raise them if necessary.

- ☑ Consider an umbrella liability policy.

- ☑ Decide whether to keep comprehensive and collision coverage.

- ☑ Drop any other unnecessary coverage.

- ☑ Raise your deductible if necessary.

- ☑ Make sure you're getting all available breaks.

- ☑ Shop for coverage at least every three years.

Property insurance

- ☑ If you're a renter, get renter's insurance.

- ☑ Review your liability limits and raise them if necessary.

- ☑ Consider an umbrella liability policy.

- ☑ Make sure you have replacement-cost coverage for your home and its contents.

- ☑ Review your coverage amounts to make sure they're adequate; raise them if necessary.

- ☑ Raise your deductibles.

- ☑ Investigate catastrophic coverage and buy it if necessary.

- ☑ Inventory your possessions and keep the record in a safe place.

- ☑ Shop around for coverage at least every three years.

Health and disability insurance

- ☑ If your employer offers coverage, evaluate your options and sign up if you haven't already.

- ☑ If you don't have insurance, investigate individual policies.

Life insurance

- ☑ Evaluate your need for life insurance and evaluate your options.

- ☑ Get rate quotes from several companies.

- ☑ Buy appropriate coverage.

- ☑ Check premiums every few years to see if you could get less expensive coverage by switching policies.

7

Buying Homes and Cars

Housing and transportation are the two biggest outlays for the typical American household. Overspending on either, or both, can put your finances seriously out of whack.

But it happens all the time. Lenders are more willing today to overload consumers with debt, and too many consumers focus solely on monthly payments—without understanding all the other costs that these big purchases involve.

We'll start with what you need to know about buying a house, and then we'll move on to what to do about your wheels.

When You're Ready to Buy a Home

Homeownership isn't the American Dream. It's the American reality. Nearly 7 out of 10 American households own their own homes. Homeownership is also (rightly) associated with wealth in the United States; the median net worth for homeowners was $184,700 in 2004, according to the Federal Reserve's Survey of Consumer Finances. For renters, it was just $4,050.

Net Worth of Homeowners Versus Renters

	Homeowners	Renters
All Households	$184,700	$4,050
Age 20 to 29	$58,770	$2,690
Age 30 to 39	$87,950	$5,500
Age 40 to 49	$185,700	$5,390
Age 50 to 59	$277,750	$4,220

Source: Federal Reserve's Survey of Consumer Finances, 2004

But homeownership isn't for everyone in all circumstances. There are plenty of bad reasons to buy a home, including these:

- **"It's a great investment."** Sometimes, in some markets, you'll do quite well. Most times, in most markets, the costs of buying, maintaining, and improving a home will offset much of the appreciation you'll get.

- **"I need the tax break."** The deductions you get for paying mortgage interest can make buying a home more affordable— that's why Congress instituted the break in the first place, to encourage homeownership. But to buy a home solely for the tax break is kind of silly. Every $1 you pay in mortgage interest gets you, at most, a 35-cent federal tax break (and usually much less because it depends on your tax bracket). When else would you pay a buck just to get back 35 cents?

- **"I'm tired of throwing money away on rent."** You're not really throwing money away—you're buying flexibility. You can move without the heavy expenses of selling a home (which typically include paying 5 to 7 percent of the house's selling price in real estate commissions), and in many markets, you'll pay less every month than if you owned a similar space.

Some folks tout the benefits of "leverage" in owning a home. Simply put, leverage means being able to use borrowed money to benefit (hopefully) from the appreciation of an asset. Let's say you buy a home for $200,000 with a 10% down payment, or $20,000. In the subsequent year, the price appreciates 6%, or $12,000. Your down payment has just "earned" a 60% return in one year. Congratulations!

Of course, this analysis ignores the interest you paid on the borrowed money, and all the costs you incurred to insure, repair, maintain and cover the taxes on said property. After those are taken into account, the benefits of leverage shrink considerably.

The idea that leverage alone is a good reason to buy a home also ignores the fact that leverage works both ways.

Let's say housing prices don't climb in the year after you buy, but instead drop by 6%. Your equity in the home shrinks from $20,000 to just $8,000. If you had to sell, you'd probably lose money after paying real estate agents' sales commissions.

I'm not saying you should remain a renter forever—far from it. Most people want to own their own walls at some point. Just make sure you can agree with each of the following statements before you take the leap:

- **"I plan to stay put for a while."** In a normal market, it can take three to five years for prices to rise enough to offset the costs of buying and selling a home. When a real estate market suffers a recession, you may have to wait a decade or more.

- **"I really want to own my own home."** Homeownership can be expensive and a hassle; no more calling the landlord to deal with an overflowing toilet at 2 a.m. Given the realities, what your parents, your friends, or your accountant think you should do isn't important; what matters is that *you* want to buy.

- **"I can afford it."** Being able to truly afford the home you want to buy has three major components: you can scrape together a down payment of at least 5%; you can manage the monthly payments required by a 30-year, fixed-rate loan (even if you ultimately choose another type of mortgage); and after the purchase is completed you have enough money left in the bank to cover your next three mortgage payments.

As I write this, people across the country are losing their homes because they used exotic or ill-advised mortgages to buy houses they really couldn't afford. Some had no idea what they were getting into and relied on bad advice; others understood but discounted the risks.

If you want to keep the home you buy, don't stretch too far to get it. If the only way you can afford the home you want is with an adjustable-rate or interest-only loan—well, then you probably can't afford that home.

The Home-Buying Timeline

Buying a home is a complicated process that involves plenty of research and decision making. It helps to get a head start. The following timeline is an ideal; you may not be able to start preparing a full year in advance, but you should try to go through all the steps anyway.

One Year Before You Want to Buy: Get Your Credit Reports and FICO Credit Scores, Pay Down Toxic Debt, and Build Up Savings

Your FICO (Fair Isaac Corporation) scores help determine the rate and terms you'll get on your mortgage, and your scores are based on the information in your credit reports. (There are many different credit-scoring formulas, but the vast majority of mortgage lenders use FICOs, so those are the scores you want to see.) You can buy your reports and your scores from MyFico.com for about $50.

Errors in your credit reports can force you to pay higher interest rates or even keep you from getting the loan you want, so peruse your reports for any accounts that aren't yours and any negative information that's older than seven years (except for bankruptcies, which can remain for 10 years). If you want detailed help on improving your scores, check out my book, *Your Credit Score: How to Fix, Improve and Protect the 3-Digit Number that Shapes Your Financial Future*. The following are the three keys to getting and keeping a good score when you're getting ready for a big purchase:

- Pay all your bills on time.

- Pay down your credit card and other revolving debt.

- Don't open or close any new accounts.

If you haven't already, you should try to pay off any "toxic debt" you owe, including credit card debts and payday loans. Then start chunking away cash so you can make at least a 5 percent down payment.

(What if you can't pay off your toxic debt and save enough for a down payment by the time you want to buy a home? Some would encourage you to go ahead anyway, but for your financial sanity, I suggest waiting until you accomplish these tasks. As I've said before, homeownership is often expensive and will just deepen your debt woes if you don't have your spending under control.)

Six Months Out: Review Your Mortgage Options, Start Calculating What You Can Afford, and Create Your New Budget

There are so many different mortgage possibilities that I've dealt with them in the next section. But here's the easy version: if you plan to stay in the home for 10 years or more, pick a 30-year fixed-rate loan. If not, pick a hybrid loan that's fixed for however long you plan to own the home (3, 5, or 7 years, typically) before becoming adjustable.

Once you know the type of mortgage you want, you can use one of the many "how much can I buy?" calculators on the Web to give you an idea of your price range. (There's a good one at LendingTree.com, and I also like MSN Money's Home Affordability Calculator.) When in doubt, go for a little less house than you think you can afford; capping your home costs will help you pay for other important expenses, like retirement. One financial planner I respect encourages her clients to limit their combined mortgage, property taxes, and homeowners' insurance payments so that they consume no more than 25 percent of their gross incomes.

Once you have a handle on how much your home is likely to cost, *create a budget that reflects those costs and start living with it.* Living as if you already owned the home can help you get used to the expenditures that will be required once you actually purchase the house, and it can give you early warning of any problems.

Three Months Out: Find a Good Real Estate Agent and Start Researching Neighborhoods

Having a real estate pro is helpful for first-time buyers and others who are intimidated by the home buying process. Just remember that only you, and not the agent or a lender, can say how much home you can afford.

Two Months Out: Get Preapproved for a Mortgage and Start Touring

A *preapproval* is a firm commitment from a lender to give you a loan. It matters a lot more to sellers than a mere *prequalification*, which is a mere indication of what a lender might give you (with no promises). Once your offer for a home is accepted, you can shop around for the best rates and terms.

Picking the Right Mortgage

"Only an idiot would get a 30-year fixed-rate loan."

A young mortgage broker once emailed me to explain why the most traditional of modern mortgages was a bad idea. Nobody, he explained, lived in a home longer than seven years, so locking in a rate for 30 was overkill. Even locking in for five years was ridiculous, since interest rates (in his short experience, anyway) only went down. And why should someone pay down principal, as traditional loans required? Why not just pay the interest and let the market build your equity for you, since real estate prices only go up?

Except that sometimes home prices go down and interest rates go up. And many smart folks try to stay in their homes a lot longer than seven years, since selling and moving often eat up 10 percent of a home's selling value.

Sometimes, despite all the mortgage innovations of the past two decades, the traditional, 30-year, fixed-rate mortgage is best.

Here are its biggest advantages.

- **Fixed rate, fixed payments**—There are few surprises with a 30-year fixed-rate loan. You know exactly what the payment will be each month. Since so many of the other costs of homeownership—maintenance, repairs, insurance, taxes—can be either unpredictable or out of your control, it can be nice to have one cost you know won't change.

- **Inflation is your friend**—Although the dollar amount of your payment won't change, it typically becomes easier to cover as years go by and your income increases. For many families, that's a blessing, since as we age other expenses often come along that require big outlays: college educations for the kids, caring for a parent, saving for retirement. Having your house payment take less of a chunk of your income over time can free up cash for those other costs.

- **You build equity**—Each payment you make is actually two: part of the money goes toward paying the interest on the loan, while the other portion reduces the amount that you owe the lender. These so-called principal payments help you build equity in your home until, after the last payment, you own your house free and clear. In the meantime, you're building up a financial cushion of equity that you may be able to tap in an emergency.

- **Built-in protection**—You're protected if rates go up, since your fixed rate can't change. But you can still benefit if rates go down, since you can always refinance. (Refinancing simply means paying off your old, higher rate loan with a new, lower-rate one.) In the old days, refinancing was pretty expensive and often had to wait until rates dropped one-and-a-half or two percentage points before refinancing made sense; but in these days of greater competition and streamlined processes, swapping your old loan for a new one might be justified if rates drop less than a point.

You don't get something for nothing in the financial world, though, and 30-year loans do have their drawbacks. The biggest drawback, for many: the monthly payments are generally higher for 30-year fixed-rate loans than those available for most other loan options, at least at the start.

Interest rates on 30-year fixed loans are typically higher than for other loan choices, too; you pay a premium for the security of knowing your payment won't change. Some people believe that premium is too high, particularly if you plan to move or refinance your home in a few years.

Then there's the issue of building equity. There are those who believe it isn't really necessary, that your home will appreciate over time and build equity for you. There are others who believe the opposite: they don't think 30-year loans build equity fast enough, and they prefer shorter-term mortgages.

Here are some of the most common types of mortgages other than 30-year fixed-rate loans and the advantages and disadvantages of each.

Adjustable-Rate Mortgages (ARMs)

Adjustable means the rate and payment on your loan can change. How often and how much depend on the terms of your loan. Adjustable rates typically come with caps that limit how much your payment can increase in a year and over the life of your loan, but your payment could still climb substantially if interest rates rise. The reward for this risk is that you typically start out with a low "teaser" rate than can substantially lower your initial payments or allow you to buy a bigger home. *ARMs can be a solution for folks who only plan to live in the home for a few years and who can afford the higher payments if they come.*

Hybrid Mortgages

Hybrid mortgages are fixed for a time—typically 3, 5 or 7 years—before becoming adjustable. Because lenders aren't locking in a rate for the life of the loan, you can typically get a somewhat lower interest rate than what you'd pay for a 30-year fixed-rate loan. *Hybrids can be a good solution for people who are pretty sure they're going to move before or shortly after the fixed period ends.*

Interest-Only Mortgages

With these loans, you pay only interest for the first few years. The interest rate may be fixed, adjustable, or a hybrid of the two (fixed for a few years before switching to adjustable). When the initial interest-only period is over, you must start paying down principal, which usually means sharply higher payments. People with high but variable incomes often like these loans because they can use their bonuses or commissions to make big principal payments and make a lower monthly payment the rest of the time. If you don't make extra payments, though, you're not building equity. If housing prices don't increase or if they fall, you could be left with little or no equity or even negative equity (owing more than the house is worth). *Interest-only mortgages can be a workable choice for sophisticated borrowers with substantial resources.* If it's the only way you can afford the house you want, though, you can't really afford that house.

Option ARMs

BusinessWeek magazine dubbed these "nightmare mortgages" with good cause. The typical option mortgage not only carries an adjustable rate, but also an adjustable payment. You can choose to make the full payment, the full payment plus an extra payment toward principal, an interest-only payment, or a "minimum" payment that doesn't even cover the interest you owe. Any unpaid interest is tacked on to the principal of your loan, a process known as *negative amortization.* In other words, your loan balance can get bigger over time, putting you in a terrible position if you need to sell the house and you owe more than it's worth. You can't get away with making the minimum payments forever, though; at some point the loan will "reset" so that you start paying principal. When that happens, your payment could double or triple, really pushing your finances to the wall. These loans can technically make sense for very sophisticated borrowers with plenty of cash who want to put that money to work in other investments but who can yank it out to pay off the loan if interest rates turn against them. *For most, though, these loans carry far more risk than rewards.*

15-Year Mortgages

If you paid off a traditional loan for 30 years, the total amount you'd pay would be more than twice the amount you originally borrowed. Someone who borrows $250,000 at 6 percent interest to buy a home, for example, would make payments totaling $539,567 over the 30-year life of the loan.

That's a lot of interest to pay. Shortening the loan term not only results in a lower interest rate, but a lot more of each payment goes toward paying down the principal and, as a result, you pay *a lot* less interest over time.

Comparing 30-Year and 15-Year Mortgages
(Amount Borrowed: $250,000)

Term	30 Years	15 Years
Interest rate	6.00%	5.75%
Monthly payment	$1,498.88	$2,076.03
Initial principal payment*	$248.88	$878.11
Initial interest payment*	$1,250.00	$1,197.92
Total interest paid	$289,595.47	$123,684.54

Amount of the first payment that goes toward principal and interest, respectively.

So why doesn't everyone grab one of these loans? The bigger monthly payments are one reason. In this example, the payment on the 15-year loan is nearly 40 percent more than on a comparable 30-year loan.

Those big payments, even if you can afford them, tend to limit your financial flexibility. You simply have less money available for other expenses.

With a 30-year loan, by contrast, you can always make additional principal payments if you want to reduce your balance, but if money is tight, you can stick to the lower, regular payment. You can't pay less on a 15-year loan unless you want to risk foreclosure.

Also most people have better things to do with their money than pay off their mortgages quickly. They should be saving for retirement, taking advantage of available workplace plans like 401(k)s, and saving in other tax-deferred accounts. They should be paying off any other, expensive debt, like credit cards, if they have it. And they should have a substantial emergency fund, preferably worth at least three months' worth of expenses. Only after those financial bases are covered should they think about paying off the mortgage.

WHY SHOULDN'T I PREPAY MY MORTGAGE?

Most of those who argue against paying off your mortgage early point out that you can get better returns in the stock market with the money you'd be using to pay off a low-rate, deductible mortgage.

Many advocates of prepaying a mortgage say that they're happier with a 4 to 6 percent guaranteed return (which is what you get from paying down a home loan) than taking chances in the volatile stock market.

This stocks versus mortgage argument is way too narrow, though. There's a lot more at stake here.

Retirement savings need to be a top priority for most folks, and most of your retirement options are "use it or lose it." If you don't contribute enough to your 401(k) to get the maximum company match, for example, you're missing out for good on that free money. (The typical plan matches each dollar you contribute with 50 cents from the company, for an instant 50 percent return.)

Other accounts, like the Roth IRA, have annual contribution limits. If you miss an opportunity to fund these accounts, you can't go back later and make up for lost time. (Some accounts do allow larger contributions for people 50 and over, but they're typically not big enough to offset the returns you lost from not making sufficient contributions earlier in your life.)

Clearly, you shouldn't think about prepaying a mortgage until you're saving sufficiently for retirement and taking full advantage of your retirement account options. For most people, this means contributing 10 to 15 percent of their gross incomes, getting the full company match in workplace plans, and contributing as much as possible to a Roth IRA.

Also you shouldn't pay off low-rate, deductible debt like a mortgage until you've retired other, higher-rate debt—especially credit cards.

In addition, you need to make sure you have sufficient insurance coverage before prepaying a mortgage. That means adequate life, health, disability, home, and auto insurance.

Finally, if you have children and want them to go to college, you probably should be saving for their education.

If, once you've covered all those bases, you still want to pay off your mortgage early, then you have my blessing. Most people, though, will have all they can handle financially meeting those other goals.

40-Year Mortgages

You might think that stretching out the loan term from 30 years to 40 years might make a loan more affordable, but in reality it doesn't.

The payments are only slightly lower on the 40-year loan (5 percent less in our example). But the extra 10 years of payments really jack up the cost over time: the interest paid over 40 years is nearly 50 percent higher than for the 30-year loan. *Some people might use these loans to qualify for a slightly more expensive home than they would get otherwise, but for most people, the loans offer little benefit.*

Comparing 30-Year and 40-Year Mortgages
(Amount Borrowed: $250,000)

Term	30-Year	40-Year
Interest rate	6.00%	6.25%
Monthly payment	$1,498.88	$1,419.35
Initial principal payment*	$248.88	$117.27
Initial interest payment*	$1,250.00	$1,302.08
Total interest paid	$289,595.47	$431,287.00

Final Thoughts on Mortgages

Now that you know your options, here are some final thoughts.

- **Rates and terms may vary**—Although major mortgage lenders try to stay competitive with each other, rates, fees, and terms can vary from loan to loan. Check out the real estate tutorials at MSN.com and the Mortgage Professor (www.mtgprofessor.com) so you can be a smart shopper. If your credit is troubled or you want extra hand-holding through this process, consider finding an experienced mortgage broker to help you sort through your options. (The National Association of Mortgage Brokers at www.namb.org can offer referrals.)

- **Set your own limits**—Lenders are often willing to give you a bigger loan than you can comfortably repay. Make sure whatever mortgage you get gives you enough financial room to save for retirement, take a vacation now and then, and pursue your other goals. Try to make sure your housing costs—your mortgage, taxes, and insurance—don't consume more than 25 percent of your gross income.

- **Know your comfort zone**—People are comfortable with different levels of risk. Don't be ashamed of wanting more security than your neighbor, brother-in-law, or broker might demand from their loans.

- **Refinance when it makes sense**—There's no ironclad rule about when you should swap your current fixed-rate loan for a new one. Generally, though, you'll want the savings from the new rate to offset the costs of the refinance in 18 months or less. You can find calculators on the Internet that will help you run the numbers; try the one at Bankrate.com.

- **But don't count on being able to refinance out of trouble**—Interest rates may rise, housing prices may fall, or your credit may take a hit that leaves you unable to get the best rates. Pick a loan that you can live with for as long as you expect to own the home.

The Smart Way to Buy Cars

The "Your Money" message board at MSN attracts a lot of posts from folks who are struggling with their budgets. Many people are frustrated because they've cut their expenses every way they can imagine, but they're still running short of cash every month.

As soon as they post their monthly expenses, the culprit often becomes obvious. It's sitting in their driveway.

Credit counselors say it's not unusual for their most cash-strapped customers to have car payments that eat up 15 percent or even 20 percent of their salaries. Some middle-class families struggle with not one but two $400 to $500 monthly payments.

There are other signs of vehicular budget-slaughter.

- **Spending on cars is rising even as incomes remain flat**— Average transportation spending grew more than 12 percent between 1999 and 2005, according to the U.S. Bureau of Labor Statistics, significantly outpacing inflation. Since median incomes didn't grow at all during that period, higher transportation spending meant many people had to cut back elsewhere or go deeper into debt to cover the cost.

- **More than 80 percent of car loans are for terms longer than four years**—This is according to Edmunds.com, a car research site that tracks loan terms. These long loans mean people build equity in their cars far more slowly than when the average loan was two or three years. Slow equity building

means borrowers stay "upside down" on their vehicles—
owing more than they're worth—for three years or more on
the typical purchase.

- **Many people don't pay off their last car before getting
  their next one**—One out of four—25.6 percent—of cars that
  are financed includes debt rolled over from a previous vehicle, Edmunds.com said. The average amount of negative
  equity in these deals was more than $4,000. Not only does
  that mean more years spent "upside down," but buyers who
  roll over debt have to pay higher interest rates as well.

What's the big deal about being upside down on a car? There are two big dangers. One is that your car will be totaled or stolen. If that happens, the payment from your insurance company typically won't be enough to pay off your
loan. Most insurance only pays the current market value of the car. If you're
upside down, that could be substantially less than you owe.

The other danger is that you won't be able to afford the payments but
won't be able to get rid of the car, either. In other words, you'll be stuck.

With other areas of your budget, you can usually find ways to trim. To cut
spending on food, for example, all you have to do is eat out less, shop grocery
store sales, and bring your lunch to work. If your utility bills are too high, you
can disconnect your cable or satellite TV service, drop a phone line, or turn
down the thermostat. Even a too-expensive rent or mortgage payment isn't
necessarily a crisis; you can take in a roommate or move somewhere cheaper.

With cars, though, your options quickly dwindle once you've signed on
the dotted line. You have to make the payments and insure it. Selling it to buy
something cheaper may not be a viable option if you owe more on the car than
it's worth; you would have to come up with the difference in cash, and you'd
still need to find some way to get to work. A too-expensive lease has similar
disadvantages; you can't turn the car back into the dealer without paying a
heavy penalty.

Why We Overspend on Cars

We could lay all the blame at the feet of car salespeople who are experts in
manipulating consumers into paying too much for cars and for financing, but
that's only part of the story. We help plant the seeds of our own destruction
by doing the following:

- **Viewing a car as a "need" rather than a "want"**—We often forget we have alternatives, including public transportation, car pools and shared-car arrangements like ZipCar and FlexCar. A car can come pretty close to a need in rural areas or when your job doesn't allow you to car pool, but even then, you have a lot of choice about what to buy (and how often to replace the car you have). You never "need" a new car—there are plenty of good used cars available that cost less. You also don't "need" to trade in a car because "it's too old" or "it has too many miles on it." The only time you need to replace a vehicle is when you have no good alternatives for transportation and the car itself has become unreliable or unsafe.

  The right way—Consider your alternatives. One way to frame the question: isn't there something else I would rather do with $8,000 a year, which is what the average U.S. household spends on a car? Can I live without a car or with one less car (if yours is a multi-car household)? Can I keep my current car going a little while longer? If you drive each car for at least ten years, you will save literally hundreds of thousands of dollars on vehicle purchases over your lifetime. Buying two- or three-year-old cars instead of new ones will save you tens of thousands of dollars more, since most cars lose a big chunk of their value in the first few years. Let someone else take that depreciation hit.

- **Using a car as a status symbol**—Ever heard the phrase, "You are what you drive?" It's baloney, of course—there's far more to you as a human being than what you park in your driveway. But car manufacturers spend a heck of a lot of money on advertising trying to convince you otherwise, and way too many people fall for it.

  The right way—Think about the ultimate status symbol, which is financial independence. Do you really want to have to work longer and harder to support a hunk of metal? Some of you car lovers may be willing to make the sacrifice, but many people have more important goals to attain.

- **Buying or leasing cars based on the monthly payment**— Unfortunately, too many people get manipulated into overspending on cars because the only factor they care about is the monthly payment. A $400 monthly payment over four years will cost you $19,200, while a $400 monthly payment over six years will cost you $28,800—a big difference. Car dealerships try to get you focused on the monthly payment and then stretch out the loan term so you'll sign up for a more expensive car and line their financing department's pockets with more interest.

Leasing is another losing proposition. You can make an argument that it's better to lease than to buy and trade in cars every two or three years, but only people with money to burn should consider doing either. If you want to make the most of your money, you'll buy good, preferably used cars and own them at least 10 years.

The right way—Don't lease cars and try not to finance cars for more than four years. Once you've paid off the car, save that monthly payment in cash toward your next vehicle. If you drive the car for at least four more years, you could easily pay cash for the next one.

- **Forgetting to factor in all the costs**—The monthly payment is just the start of the costs you'll pay for a vehicle. You also have to shell out for taxes, insurance, gas, maintenance, and repairs. Then there's *depreciation*, which is a fancy word for the steady drop in your car's value. You don't pay for depreciation as it happens, but you'll pay when you're ready to trade this car in for the next one. Most cars, according to Edmunds.com, will cost you at least twice the initial purchase price during the first five years of ownership.

  The right way—If you're trying to decide whether you can afford the monthly costs of a car, check out Edmunds.com's "True Cost to Own" feature.

- **Assuming you can afford a car because your loan or lease got approved**—It shouldn't be a shocker by now, but lenders don't really care if you can afford a payment. They're just betting that enough of their customers will make their payments to offset the few who default, and they don't particularly care what happens to your finances in the meantime.

  The right way—Decide for yourself what you can afford. In general, your *total* ongoing car costs—including payments, registration, insurance, gas, and maintenance—should consume less than 15 percent of your gross monthly income. But you may need to spend less depending on your other expenses; use the budget guidelines in Chapter 2, "Take Charge of Your Spending," to help you decide.

- **Failing to research before walking on to a car lot**—Many buyers do only cursory research before stumbling on a car lot "to look around." They might as well paint big red targets on their back. Good car salespeople know exactly how to herd folks like this into overpaying for cars, pressuring them to grab a "deal" before it "expires," paying them ridiculously small amounts for their trade-ins, loading them up with unnecessary add-ons, and rushing them into too-expensive loans.

  The right way—Smart buyers use the Internet to research the vehicles that might suit them. They decide in advance what features they want. Once they've narrowed the field, they get detailed car price reports from Consumer Reports so they know how to make a smart offer. (Another good source of bargaining information is the Edmunds.com book *Strategies for Smart Car Buyers*.) If they have to finance a car, they know their credit scores and what interest rates they deserve based on those scores. Then they arrange financing in advance, often through a credit union.

What to Do if You've Already Overspent

As I mentioned earlier, your options once you've overspent are few. You can sell the car if you owe less than the car is worth. If you owe more, you need to come up with the extra cash or convince the lender to let you pay off the balance over time (and most lenders won't bite).

You may be able to lower your payments by refinancing. If you purchased the car new, the lender may be willing to extend your loan term. If not, you might be able to refinance with another lender if you have some equity in the car.

Another option, repossession, is a terrible idea unless you have no other choice. Even if you voluntarily hand the keys back to the dealer, repossession will trash your credit scores, and you'll still be on the hook to pay off the loan (plus the costs of repossession, which can be substantial).

The best choice is usually to "drive out of the loan," which means you continue making the payments, trimming the rest of your budget as necessary. Once you've got the car paid off, you continue driving it until you've saved up the money to buy another vehicle or at least bring a 20 percent down payment to the bargaining table.

One other precaution you should take if you are "upside down" on an auto loan or lease: buying so-called "gap" insurance. These policies pay the difference between what you owe and what your auto insurer would pay for a stolen or totaled car. You typically can purchase gap insurance through your dealership or auto finance company, although that's typically the most expensive choice. Try to get it instead from your auto insurer, if it's offered, or from another insurance carrier. If you're buying from an unknown carrier, first check its ratings with A.M. Best, Standard & Poor's, or TheStreet.com ratings.

Your Checklist

Here's your list of things to do from this chapter.

Before you buy a house

- ☑ Review (and improve) your credit reports and credit scores.

- ☑ Pay off toxic debt, such as credit card balances and payday loans.

- ☑ Review your mortgage options and calculate what you can afford to buy.

- ☑ Make a budget that reflects your projected home's costs and live with it for several months.

- ☑ Get preapproved for a mortgage.

- ☑ Shop for rates and terms once your offer has been approved.

Before you buy a car

- ☑ Consider all your alternatives, including keeping the vehicle you have or living without a car.

- ☑ Consider buying used.

- ☑ Own your cars for at least 10 years; don't finance them for more than 4 years.

- ☑ Limit total vehicle costs, including payments, gas, maintenance, and insurance, to no more than 15 percent of your gross income.

8

When You Need Help

In the previous chapters, I've shown easy ways that you can set up your finances, invest for retirement, and buy insurance on your own.

But many people long for a little hand-holding when it comes to finances. And there's nothing wrong with that.

In fact, there are some areas of your finances—taxes and estate planning in particular—where professional help can be indispensable. This chapter discusses when you need a pro in these areas and how to find one.

Professional help also comes in handy when you want a second opinion on your investment portfolio or a review of your overall financial situation to make sure that you're on the right track and haven't missed anything important. As you approach retirement, such a review becomes absolutely essential, since many of the decisions you'll be facing—when to take Social Security, how to tap your retirement funds, whether to buy long-term care insurance—are irreversible, easy to mess up, and best made with a financial planner's input.

Here's how to find good help.

How to Find a Financial Planner

There are hundreds of thousands of people passing themselves off as financial planners in the United States today. Very few are what they seem.

Anyone can call herself a financial planner or financial advisor. There are no education, experience, or ethics requirements for using those terms.

Furthermore, most of the people who want to offer you advice *are not legally obligated to put your interests before their own.* They can sell you overpriced, poorly performing investment products—even when less expensive, better-performing ones are available—because they get fatter commissions or other incentives from the inferior investment.

Sometimes there's more at stake than just the advisor's paychecks. Some insurance companies take away their agents' health insurance coverage if those agents don't push enough of the companies' products. I feel sorry for agents who have to choose between recommending a suitable product and protecting their families' health, but I feel sorrier for their clients.

You also shouldn't assume that someone who works for a bank, brokerage, or insurance company is necessarily well educated about personal finance. Many times, the only education they've received is about their companies' products. If they haven't taken it upon themselves to pursue a comprehensive financial planning education, they may have no idea that alternative products or strategies exist—or that the information their companies have been feeding them isn't accurate.

I'd even be leery of using an advisor simply based on a friend or relative recommendation. After all, how savvy are your friends and relatives about finances? Would they recognize an unqualified or unethical person? Did they perform a background check themselves before hiring this advisor? There are way too many *affinity frauds* out there—scam artists who convince a few influential people in a community or religious organization to invest with them and then get those influential people to recommend them to others.

So how do you find someone who can actually help, rather than harm, your finances? The following sections should put you on the right path.

Insist on a CFP

The Certified Financial Planner (CFP) mark has emerged as the gold-standard credential for the financial planning profession. Someone who's a Certified Financial Planner has gone through a comprehensive education process, passed a tough test, and gotten some experience under his belt. That doesn't necessarily mean he is competent or ethical, but a CFP is the minimum credential you should demand from anyone who wants to give you financial planning advice. Just as good is the PFS, or Personal Financial Specialist, which is a planning credential offered to CPAs.

Choose a Fee-Only Planner

A true *fee-only* planner is compensated only by the fees you pay, not by commissions or fees paid by other entities. Don't be confused by advisors who call themselves *fee-based*. They could be (and probably are) receiving commissions in addition to the fees that you pay. Taking commissions doesn't make someone a bad person, but it does present a pretty substantial conflict of interest. Besides, it's so last century. The smartest, most ethical, and most competent planners I know are all fee-only. Also they're willing to say, in writing, that they are "fiduciaries," which means they're obligated to put your interests ahead of their own.

Get Referrals

Those smart, ethical, competent planners I just referred to? Most are members of The National Association of Personal Financial Advisors at www.napfa. org, which represents fee-only planners and has strict experience, education, and ethics requirements. Not all NAPFA members advise middle-class folks; many of these planners require their clients to have substantial portfolios, and they tend to charge a percentage of their clients' portfolios, rather than flat or hourly fees. If you're looking for by-the-hour planning, consider referrals from The Garrett Planning Network at www.garrettplanningnetwork.com.

Ask Questions

If you've chosen a fee-only CFP, many of the important questions have been answered. But there are a few more things you should know. How long has the planner been in the business? (To get a CFP, a planner needs at least three years of experience, but I'd be more comfortable with someone who's been planning professionally for at least five years.) What are his areas of specialization? What is his typical client like? You probably want a planner who has experience working with others in situations similar to yours.

Check Their Background

Ask for Form I and Form II of their ADV, which is paperwork that advisors have to file with the Securities and Exchange Commission. These forms will show you how your advisor is paid (commissions, fees, or a combination) and recap any disciplinary history with regulators. Go a step further and check that history with the SEC (www.sec.gov), the National Association of Securities Dealers (www.nasd.com), and your state's investment regulator.

Most true financial planners prefer to look at your entire financial picture, including your spending, investment, insurance, tax, and estate situations, so that they can offer comprehensive advice. This process will involve many hours of their time and, typically, a fee that can reach thousands of dollars.

But some—particularly those you pay by the hour—are willing to limit them-selves to specific situations, such as a review of your retirement portfolio. That would allow you to get some of your burning questions answered for a few hundred dollars.

When You Need a Tax Pro

I once heard from a stay-at-home mom who was very proud of the money she saved her family in various ways, including doing their taxes herself. Then she discovered that her family of four children was eligible for child tax cred-its—credits that she had failed to claim, because she didn't know about them. She was able to amend her most recent tax returns, but you can't claim refunds after three years, so the earlier unclaimed credits were lost for good. Her sincere desire to save her family a couple hundred bucks a year wound up costing them thousands.

I discovered how truly tricky taxes could be during the 1990s when I tested various kinds of tax software as part of my newspaper reporting job. Each year, I did my taxes as many as eight times using different programs. My situation wasn't extremely complex, but I did own a home and run a free-lance business in addition to my W-2 income.

Inevitably, my tax bill would come out differently depending on the soft-ware I used. Then my tax pro did my return, and every time she found mis-takes I had made and deductions I had missed. Every year, she more than made up for her fee in an increased refund—but even if she hadn't, I would have used her just for the assurance that my taxes were being done by some-one who really and truly knew what she was doing.

Perhaps there was a time when a taxpayer with a pencil, a calculator, and a lot of patience could do a reasonably good job of completing her own return. Today, though, the U.S. tax code has gotten so complex that it could be com-pared to a really bad neighborhood: you shouldn't go there alone.

At the very least, you should be using good software, such as TurboTax or TaxCut. If you do your own taxes, you must also keep up with major new tax developments; you can buy a good annual guide like *J. K. Lasser's Your Income Tax* or *The Ernst & Young Tax Guide* and read the chapters about what's new in the tax law.

But really, most people should consider hiring a knowledgeable tax pro. It's not just smart delegation, although of course someone who lives and breathes tax law is going to do a better job with your return. But you're also providing yourself with a valuable resource during the rest of the year when tax questions pop up and you need answers.

You absolutely should hire a tax pro when any of the following conditions apply:

- **You own a business**—As complicated as personal taxes can be, business taxes are worse. Just the decision of how to conduct your business—sole proprietorship? partnership? corporation? C or S or LLC?—could drive a regular person around the bend, but CPAs handle these questions every day. A tax pro can also give you good advice about maximizing your business-related deductions, audit-proofing your returns, and picking the right retirement account. *Good business owners know how to delegate, and delegating taxes to a professional is a smart choice.*

- **You've fallen under the dreaded alternative minimum tax (AMT)**—This parallel tax system was set up to keep the wealthy from using loopholes to avoid all tax liability. Because Congress hasn't linked it to inflation, however, millions of decidedly not-wealthy folks have lost deductions and found their tax bills hiked by the AMT. You're most at risk if you have a lot of write-offs, have lots of kids, or live in a high-tax state. The good news is that you may be able to lessen the pain with smart planning, and a tax pro can help.

- **Your company has issued you stock options**—Stock options can bring you wealth, but they can also trigger all kinds of nasty surprises—including big tax bills even when your investment has lost value. You'll want a professional review of your situation before you exercise any stock options as well as follow-up afterward.

- **You've just received a notice that you're about to be audited**—Not only should you not represent yourself in an IRS audit, but you also probably shouldn't even *be* there when the auditor and your tax pro review your returns. If you do insist on coming, sit in a corner and keep your darn mouth shut.

How do you find a good tax pro? If you're looking tax savvy at an affordable price, consider hiring an *enrolled agent* (EA). These folks are licensed by the federal government and can defend you in an audit. (Many EAs, in fact, are former IRS employees.) The National Association of Enrolled Agents at www.naea.org can provide referrals.

For more complicated situations, consider a *certified public accountant* (CPA). CPAs tend to be more expensive than EAs but may offer more expertise in specific areas like corporate or international taxation. If you want a CPA with financial planning expertise, look for one who has a PFS credential. Your state CPA society can offer referrals, or you can visit the American Institute of Certified Public Accountants at www.aicpa.org.

As with financial planners, you'll want to find a tax pro who has other clients like you—with similar incomes and tax situations. You should ask not only *how much* the pro charges but also *how* they charge. (Some are happy to answer the occasional question for free, figuring it's included in your annual tax preparation fee, while others charge like lawyers—by the minute.)

There's another issue you need to assess, and for lack of a better term I call it audit compatibility.

There are plenty of gray areas in tax law—and sometimes not much enforcement. Some tax pros pride themselves on saving their clients as much money as possible, even if it means taking aggressive stances that might not survive an audit.

At the other end of the scale are those whose goal is to avoid IRS scrutiny at all costs. These folks may pass on perfectly legitimate deductions because it raises the chances of an IRS audit by a few percentage points.

Obviously, most tax pros are somewhere between these two extremes. But you'll want to make sure that wherever your pro lands on the spectrum, you're comfortable with that.

How do you determine their philosophies? It may become obvious during your introductory chat, while you're asking about their background, experience, and other clients. A tax pro who brags about the big refunds he lands his clients is probably going to be more aggressive than one who highlights her low audit rate.

If you're not clear, though, raise a thorny tax issue or two. Mention, for example, that you're considering hiring a housekeeper but don't want to hassle with paying employment taxes. The hot-rod tax pro might launch into an eager discussion of ways to keep your arrangement off the IRS's radar while the most conservative might refuse to work with you at all. Someone in between might go over all your legal alternatives, such as hiring a payroll tax service to handle the paperwork or simply using a business, like Merry Maids, that takes care of such issues for you.

Working with an Estate Planning Attorney

Every once in a while, you'll see an article about how "everybody" needs a will. It's just not true.

If you don't have children and don't care what happens to your money and possessions after you die, you don't need a will. Your state has rules for what happens to your stuff.

The thing is most of us do care.

One of my friends blithely put off creating a will, knowing that under her state's laws, her husband would inherit everything if she died. Then a married couple she knew was killed in a plane crash, and she started wondering who would inherit if she and her spouse died together. The answer, in her state, was her father—an abusive man from whom she'd been estranged for years. Suddenly, creating a will became a top priority.

Having a will is also essential if you have minor children. You need to name a guardian and set up a trust to manage any money they inherit from you. Otherwise, a court battle could erupt over their care, and their money would be turned over to them at age 18—which is way too young to handle a big lump sum of cash.

Even if you don't think you need a will, you do need three things:

- **A durable power of attorney for finances**, which allows you to name someone to make financial decisions for you if you're incapacitated

- **A durable power of attorney for health care**, which allows you to name someone to make medical decisions for you

- **A living will**, which tells your doctors what kind of end-of-life care you want if you are terminally ill and incapacitated

These documents can make an enormous difference in the quality of your life while you're still around to care.

You can create your own estate documents using software; the best by far is Quicken WillMaker, which uses an interview process to help you refine and set down your wishes. The Nolo Press book *Plan Your Estate* is another good resource to have on hand.

This do-it-yourself approach can work fine if your affairs are simple and your estate is relatively small. But you'll want to hire an estate-planning attorney to draft your documents if any of the following is true:

- **Your estate is big enough to incur federal estate taxes**— Estates worth more than $2 million in 2007 and 2008 may owe taxes; the so-called estate tax exemption will rise to $3.5 million in 2009. But you should strongly consider an estate planner's help as soon as your net worth clicks over the $1 million mark, particularly if your wealth is likely to grow in the future. Getting expert advice on minimizing taxes and probate costs can be a worthwhile investment.

- **You have a contentious family**—If anyone is likely to contest your will or start a court fight over guardianship of your child, you'll want an experienced professional to help you ward off or nullify their attempts to upend your wishes.

- **You have a special-needs child**—If your child is disabled, you'll probably want to set up a special trust and protect your assets to ensure lifetime care. This can be an incredibly complicated area of the law, and your chosen professional needs to be up-to-date with all the latest state and federal developments.

If your estate is complex enough to require an attorney, it's probably worthwhile to seek out one who specializes in estate planning, rather than a general practitioner. One place to check is with your state's bar association to see if it certifies estate-planning specialists. (Some states do; others don't.)

Another good source for referrals is other attorneys. If you know a lawyer who you like and trust, ask whom she would recommend. Doctors and other professionals may be able to offer recommendations. So might your tax pro or financial planner.

An estate-planning attorney's background, education, and experience are all important. But, so too, is your rapport with your attorney. Before you sign up, take some time to chat about your various estate-planning concerns. Does the attorney answer your questions in a way you can understand? If you need clarification, does she provide it? Estate law can be dauntingly complex, but a good attorney will be your guide. She won't make you feel like an idiot for your ignorance or try to waive off your concerns with a "don't worry your pretty little head" attitude.

The advice you're getting won't come cheap. Although an attorney can draft a simple will for a few hundred bucks, more complicated estate plans will cost a couple thousand dollars—and up. Take the time to find someone who gives you your money's worth.

DO YOU REALLY NEED A LIVING TRUST?

A *living trust* is an estate-planning document that does every-thing a will can do, plus it allows an estate to bypass probate, the court process that otherwise follows death.

In some states, like California, probate is a real nightmare. It can take more than a year for the typical estate to complete probate, and the fees involved can eat up 3 percent or more of the assets involved. Your heirs typically must wait until the long process is over to receive their inheritances; guardians for minor children and those running your business must submit to court oversight and approval of their actions.

In other states, probate takes just a few months, and costs are relatively small, making the $2,000 to $3,000 cost of setting up a living trust harder to justify for modest estates.

To determine whether a living trust is right for you, I'd encour-age you to read the Nolo Press book *Plan Your Estate*, as well as *8 Ways to Avoid Probate* by Mary Randolph.

In general, though, the younger you are and the less you own, the less a living trust makes sense. You may be able to avoid probate through other means, such as owning property in joint tenancy and using "pay on death" designations for financial accounts. If you're in your 50s or older and have substantial means, though, you should at least consider the benefits of a living trust.

To reduce costs, you could make this a do-it-yourself project. Nolo Press has a guide, "Make Your Own Living Trust," that includes a CD-ROM of forms to fill out. But given the potential complexities involved, I'd invest in a lawyer's help, particularly if you may someday have enough assets to incur estate taxes.

What you don't want to do is buy a cut-rate trust or boilerplate forms from a so-called "living trust mill." These outfits often try to scare older people with exaggerated horror stories about pro-bate. Their usual purpose is to get their clients to reveal details of their finances so that they can be sold overpriced annuities and other unsuitable products.

If you're going to pay someone for a trust, make sure she is a qualified estate-planning attorney and that the trust is cus-tomized for your needs.

Your Checklist

Here's your list of things to do from this chapter.

If you're looking for financial planning help:

- ☑ Insist on a CFP or PFS.
- ☑ Get referrals to fee-only planners.
- ☑ Ask about experience, cost, and typical clients.
- ☑ Do background checks.

If you're looking for tax help:

- ☑ Use software like TurboTax or TaxCut if your situation is relatively simple.
- ☑ Seek a pro's help if you own a business, are subject to AMT, are issued stock options, or are notified that you'll be audited.
- ☑ Consider enrolled agents, who can provide tax help and representation at a reasonable cost.
- ☑ Choose a CPA for more complex or specialized situations.

When you need an estate plan:

- ☑ Determine whether you need a will. Use do-it-yourself resources only if your estate is small and your situation is straightforward.
- ☑ Make sure you have powers of attorney for finances and health care decisions and a living will.
- ☑ Seek an attorney's help if you have a large or complicated estate or a contentious family.

9

Be a Savvy Shopper

Most personal finance books, including this one, spend a lot of time yakking about saving, investing, and protecting your money. Not much time is spent talking about spending (well, other than telling you to do less of it!)

But smart shopping skills are essential for anyone who wants to manage money well. And technology—particularly the Internet—has made the task easier than ever before. You can research potential purchases, check out a company's return policy and reputation, scoop up valuable discounts, and comparison shop yourself silly, all without leaving your home. I'll share some of the sites that will help you get the most for your money.

You also need a set of skills for dealing with spending that goes awry: stuff that breaks before its time, bogus charges that wind up on your bill, the customer service department from hell. I'll provide you with some strategies that can help you cope with these situations and make you more effective in getting what you want.

Sites Worth Paying For

One of the beautiful aspects of the Internet is that most of it is free. Very few sites can get away with charging for their content, so—at least for now—the vast majority of Web information is out there for the taking.

There are some sites, though, that offer knowledge worth buying. One of them is ConsumerReports.org, the Web site of the venerable independent research organization. Before you make any major purchase (and many minor ones), you should see what *Consumer Reports* has to say about the available products and how to shop for the best buy. No other site has *Consumer Reports*' reputation for objectivity and thoroughness, and its Web site is easy to use. The cost? Just $26 a year.

Another helpful site, if you're a homeowner, is Angie's List. Trying to find a good, reliable, honest carpenter, plumber, electrician, or handyman? Benefit from the advice and feedback of thousands of other homeowners by checking out who's recommended on Angie's List. From air duct cleaners to wrought iron workers, you can get recommendations on who to hire and who to avoid. Membership costs about $20 for a single month or about $65 for a year.

Price Comparison Sites

You need never wonder if you're getting a bargain on a purchase, online or off; with price-comparison Web sites, you'll know.

Add a few of these to the "favorites" list on your browser:

- Google Product Search (formerly known as Froogle) (www.google.com/products)

- MSN (http://shopping.msn.com)

- Yahoo (http://shopping.yahoo.com)

- Pricegrabber (www.pricegrabber.com)

- MySimon (www.mysimon.com)

- ShopLocal (www.shoplocal.com)

This last shop keeps track of sales in your local area, "online and in-store."

You'll find links to product reviews and opinions from other consumers. Other sites you might want to check out include Epinions.com, Amazon.com (which includes users' reviews for a wide range of products, not just books), and TripAdvisor.com for travel.

Internet Shopping 101

The sites I've mentioned so far can help you even if you never make a purchase online. But since you probably will do a fair amount of shopping on the Internet, let's review the basics.

Keep Your Defenses Up

Anyone who cruises the Internet using a high-speed connection should have a firewall, which is a barrier to help keep out destructive software programs and hackers. If you're not sure whether you have one, consider making an appointment with a computer tech to review your system. (One fairly affordable option is Circuit City's The Geek Squad.) You also need antivirus software, such as McAfee Virus Scan or Norton AntiVirus. Be sure to keep the software updated (the programs will nudge you periodically to download new "pattern files," or bits of programming that detect new problems) and run scans at least weekly. Also essential is good antispyware software, such as Lavasoft's Ad-Aware, available for free at www.lavasoftusa.com. Like antivirus software, you need to update and run antispyware regularly. (Spyware are programs that keep track of your movements on the Web, reporting to the companies or hackers that inflicted it on your machine without your knowledge.) Keeping your defenses strong can prevent your computer from being hijacked and block the bad guys from stealing your private personal and financial information.

Stick with Companies You Know

It's a good idea, particularly when you're new to Internet buying, to shop with companies whose reputations you know and trust. If you do contemplate a purchase from an unknown buyer, such as a company or person who sells on an auction site like eBay, carefully review feedback from other buyers—particularly the most recent feedback. Some scam artists build a strong reputation using small sales; then they rip off customers with big sales before disappearing into the ether.

Review the Privacy Policy

Some sites do a great job of keeping your private information private; others try to market every scrap of information they can find out about you. Opt out of such "information sharing" if you're given a choice; if not, choose another company with which to do business. Also pay close attention to any check boxes that pop up giving the company permission to send you advertising; opt out of those, as well.

Review the Return Policy

Before buying anything, check out how returns are handled. Some online stores, like L. L. Bean's, are famous for their no-hassle returns. Other sites charge hefty "restocking" fees and stick you with shipping charges, *even when they make a mistake*. Forewarned is forearmed.

Look for the Padlock

Once you're ready to buy, you should be transferred from the online store's regular site to a secure site where transaction information is encrypted and made safe for Internet travel. You'll know you're there when you look at the Web site address at the top of your browser window and see "https" instead of "http." Also a small padlock should appear either to the right of the address window or in the bottom-right hand part of your browser. If you don't see those things, don't enter credit card numbers or other personal information.

Use a Credit Card but Don't Let the Site "Keep" It

You may have several options for payment, including using debit cards, online payment systems like PayPal, or even electronic transfers from a bank account. But you have the most protection with a credit card. The credit card issuer can serve as a middleman in any disputes, and you have extra protection against fraud. Don't, however, take any site up on its offer to "store" your credit card information for you. While transaction information is encrypted, you can't be assured that the Web site's database of stored information is hacker-proof. Better safe than sorry.

Sites to Bookmark

Some Web sites do nothing but look for bargains on other Web sites. I warn you: these can be addictive—so addictive that one, DealNews (http://dealnews.com), used to carry the tagline "Go broke saving money."

Many of these sites specialize in featuring multilayered deals: bargains where a coupon, rebate, or free shipping can be combined with a hot sale. Recently, for example, FatWallet (www.fatwallet.com) highlighted a one-day free shipping offer on Lego sets at ToysRUs; then it dug up two sample bargains: a 103-piece Lego Duplo set for $7.49 and a Lego Star Wars Episode III V-Wing Fighter for $9.99. The site pointed out that people who used Google checkout, a method of paying for online purchases through the Google Web site, for the first time could save an additional $10.

In addition to the deals featured on its main page, FatWallet, like many of the other bargain-hunting sites, has message boards where people can post deals and tips. FatWallet and eBates (www.ebates.com) also give extra rebates to people who register and shop through their sites. (Always review a site's privacy policy before you sign up or otherwise give out personal information to make sure you're comfortable with how that information will be used.)

A few more sites to check out include Ben's Bargains (http://bensbargains.net), SlickDeals (www.slickdeals.net), and MyBargainBuddy (www.mybargainbuddy.com).

You can bookmark these sites by adding them to your Web browser's favorite list. Or, if you don't want to jump from site to site, you can have their information sent to you using really simple syndication (RSS).

RSS pulls information and headlines off various Web sites and aggregates it in one place—an RSS reader. The latest versions of Internet Explorer and Mozilla Firefox have RSS readers built in, or you can use free Web readers such as Google Reader, NewsGator, or MyYahoo. Subscribing is often as simple as clicking an orange button on the site to which you want to subscribe; the button typically has the letters RSS or XML or a dot with two arcs.

Check for Coupons

I don't make any online purchases or any big offline purchases without first checking to see if an online coupon is available. Searching can be as simple as entering the word "coupon" plus the name of the store where you're shopping into a search engine like Google. You may have to check out a few before you find a relevant, unexpired coupon, but it's typically worth the effort.

There are plenty of commercial sites, like the bargain sites listed in the previous section, that provide coupons. But I'd also encourage you to check out Alex's Coupons at www.alexscoupons.com. The site was started by the parents of a little girl with leukemia to help pay for her treatment, and it has since gone on to donate to various cancer organizations.

When You're in the Market for Real Bargains

You can save a ton of money buying gently used rather than new. Yard sales and consignment shops are a couple of places to find bargains, but the Internet can open up a much wider world of possibilities.

For example, people use Craigslist (www.craigslist.com) to find apartments, jobs, and mates, but it's also a great place to find good used stuff.

It's essentially a huge classified ad site where people hawk (just about) everything you can imagine. If you've never been to Craigslist before, you'll probably land by default in the site's San Francisco Bay listings—just click on your city or state on the right-hand portion of the page and you'll be redirected to your local site.

Freecycle.org (freecycle.org) is a site where people give away stuff. Seriously. It started because a guy in Arizona hated to see perfectly usable items wind up at the dump. At last count, there were more than 4,000 Freecycle groups with more than 3 million members, all giving and getting free stuff. (There's an etiquette to the whole thing; you're supposed to give something away before asking for something specific, and there's no guarantee you'll get what you want.)

Check out Half.com (Half.ebay.com) and Amazon.com (amazon.com) for used books, music, and movies.

A Word about Price Guarantees

Lots of stores promise to match or beat their competitors' prices. The purpose of these claims is to get you to stop shopping and buy.

The problem is that these guarantees usually come with lots of loopholes, require lots of work on your part to claim, or both.

You typically have only a short time span to spot the lower price, and you usually need to provide some sort of evidence, like an advertising circular. When you're using a travel Web site, timing is even more critical: you usually have only 24 hours, and the company's representatives have to be able to find the same lower price you did. If the lower price popped up briefly on a Web site and then disappeared, you're out of luck.

Some of the companies offering guarantees do a pretty good job of keeping their prices competitive. Other companies see a guarantee as a low-risk advertising gambit, since relatively few people will try to make a claim.

A slight variation on the low-price guarantee is a "price protection" guarantee. This promise, offered by Amazon, Best Buy, Office Max, Target, and others, offers to refund the difference if the price on an item you buy drops within a certain time after your purchase.

If you do buy online at one of the stores that has such a policy, check out Price Protectr at www.priceprotectr.com. The site promises to alert you if the cost of the item you bought drops within the stores' protected time frame.

If you plan to rely on a company's guarantee, read the fine print so you know what's involved in evoking it. Don't let a potentially empty promise be a substitute for doing your own research.

How to Be a Savvy Traveler

Americans spend more than half a trillion dollars on travel every year, but some travelers consistently get more for their money than others. These savvy consumers know a few tricks that get them good deals and free perks without spending a lot of extra money.

Among the proven strategies are these.

Be Loyal

If you travel more than sporadically, it makes sense to concentrate your business with one airline, one or two hotel chains, and one or two car rental companies. Sign up for their frequent-traveler programs, and you'll benefit from perks like free upgrades, unadvertised discounts, and free flights or stays. Concentrating your business this way also helps if you have problems, since travel providers tend to treat their frequent customers better than someone who just grabbed a low rate and has no plans to use them again.

Pick Your Site

Third-party travel sites like Expedia, Orbitz, and Travelocity can help you compare costs, but you'll typically get a slight price break (and earn more frequent-traveler points) if you book at the Web sites run directly by the airline, hotel, and car rental company. Where third-party sites really excel is in vacation packages; they often can get a combination of airfare and hotel that's cheaper than anything you'll dig up on your own.

If you really want a bargain, though, try sites like LastMinuteTravel.com or the "blind" auction sites, like Priceline.com and Hotwire.com. This is where travel providers dump seats, rooms, and cars they can't otherwise sell. You have to be flexible to use these sites; LastMinuteTravel often doesn't specify which hotel or airline is offering a particular deal and the blind auction sites never do (at least when you use the auction function). With Priceline.com and Hotwire, you specify certain perimeters—which day you want to fly and where you're going, for example—and bid a certain amount, hoping a travel provider will take you up on your offer. If the provider accepts your bid, you can get a trip at a serious discount, but you don't get to pick the airline or time of departure.

Still, you can get serious bargains. We recently nabbed a four-star hotel room in San Diego for about half the lowest rate advertised on Expedia.

Don't Stop Shopping

You probably know that travel prices change all the time, thanks to the "yield management" software companies use to try to anticipate consumer demand. (That's how two people sitting next to each other on a plane can wind up paying vastly different sums for the same flight.) If you haven't already locked in the price—by using a blind auction site, for example, or one of the nonrefundable booking options on a traveler provider's site—you might be able to find a better rate. So once you've booked a flight or a hotel room, check back periodically to see if prices have dropped. The drops have to be fairly dramatic to make rebooking a plane ticket worthwhile, since there's usually a $50 to $100 change fee, but most hotel and car reservations can be rebooked at no charge. (I rebooked one hotel room in New York three times in as many weeks, eventually chopping more than $75 off the per-night room rate.)

When Things Go Wrong

You're zipping along, master of your fate, in control of your money and your life. Then some service or piece of technology you count on stops working. Or you get charged for something you didn't buy. Or you encounter unexpected rudeness and idiocy from customer service instead of, well, customer service.

Getting satisfaction when things go wrong is part art and part science. I've been perfecting my techniques for years, and I consider myself a pretty good complainer. I've gotten free hotel rooms, free meals, and even a free laptop in recent years. I've also interviewed many on-the-frontline phone reps to find out what does and doesn't work.

Here's what you need to know the next time life throws you a curve.

Know Your Rights

It helps to understand the bare minimum you're due as a consumer. If the problem involves a credit card transaction, for example, you should read the dispute information on the back of your statement or on the issuer's Web site and follow the instructions for making a complaint. (You also may have rights under the Fair Credit Reporting Act [updated as the Fair and Accurate Credit Transactions Act] and the Fair Debt Collection Practices Act.) If your complaint involves a contract or warranty, read all the fine print. Various regulatory agencies also may have information about what you're owed. The Internet is a great resource for beefing up on state and federal laws.

Understand the System

If you knew how many customer service departments were run, you might be more sympathetic with the poor saps who have to take your calls. They face unhappy people all day long, and they're often judged on how quickly they get you off the phone, not necessarily how satisfied you are. They might even be under pressure to sell you new products and services—as if a ticked-off customer is in any mood to listen to those kind of spiels. Their problems aren't your problems, of course, but understanding the pressures they're under could help you moderate your irritation and win over possible allies.

Don't Be a Diva

Making a big fuss about a small problem won't get you very far with the typical overworked sales or customer service representative. Neither will being rude or flying into a rage, no matter how much you may have been provoked. My husband, who's an awesome negotiator and the most effective complainer I know, puts it this way: you don't have to be nice, necessarily (although I find it helps when dealing with people who are used to being screamed at). You do have to be polite. Polite, firm, reasonable people tend to get what they want a lot more often than people who are jerks.

Know What You Want

It helps to have a clear idea of the outcome or fix you want before you make your complaint. Again, you must be reasonable; it's okay to ask the dry cleaner who ruined your jacket to replace it, but it's not okay to ask for free dry cleaning for life. Also be concise, both in describing the problem and in outlining the solution you want. It's easy to tune out someone who keeps nattering on about unimportant details.

Get to a Human—Fast

I'm convinced that some companies' voice mail systems were designed by the CIA as an experiment to see how quickly sane people could be driven mad. Skip the "listen carefully for our menu options have changed" nonsense and use one of the Internet cheat sheets, such as GetHuman.com, to find the combination of numbers and symbols that will get you to a real, live person. Or skip the phone entirely and go straight to the Internet. I've had good luck using the complaint forms provided in the customer service section of many company Web sites. You typically get a response within 24 hours, and some have instant message functions that allow you to chat in real time with a human being. If that doesn't work for you, you can always head back to the phone. (One note: if you're dealing with a credit or bank account transaction, you may also want to make your complaint in writing and send a letter certified mail, return receipt requested to establish a paper trail and preserve your rights under federal law.)

Know That the Company's Problems Are Not Your Problems

Once you explain your situation, the customer-service rep may start to describe in detail why company policy won't allow her to help you. The good news: you don't have to care. The company's policies are its own internal business, while your concern is getting your problem fixed, however the company ultimately decides to do it. I was once told, at great length and by several different phone reps, why my request to have a malfunctioning laptop replaced was impossible under company policy. I persisted, rejecting every half-measure solution they tried to offer, and eventually got my new laptop.

Enlist the Rep

Here's where being nice does come in handy. If you've established some rapport with the phone rep and then hit a roadblock, ask how she would solve the problem in your shoes. Overworked, underpaid reps may relish the chance to show off their inside knowledge of the organization and help out someone who actually treated them like a human being.

Hang Up and Try Again

You may get a real loser on the phone—someone who is snotty, unhelpful, or just incompetent. You can try asking for a supervisor, but a more effective course of action could be saying goodbye, hanging up, and redialing the customer service number. You'll almost certainly get a new rep, and you can start from scratch. (I once had to try three times; somehow I got the same rude computer tech twice when dealing with a malfunctioning modem in a hotel room.)

Don't Get Worn Down

The worst customer service departments specialize in transferring you, putting you on hold, and then—oops—"accidentally" disconnecting you. That's why it's important to get names and call-back numbers of everyone you talk to and to keep notes of what was said. It's also helpful to have a portable phone and a headset so you can get other things done while you wait them out.

Move Up the Ladder

If you can't fix the problem by phone or email, you need to aim higher—and do it in writing. Send a letter (certified mail, return receipt requested) to the chief executive officer, whose name and address you'll find on the company's Web site. (Sometimes it's well-hidden, but if the company is publicly traded you'll find the information you're seeking in the "investor relations" section; check under SEC filings for Form 10-K, which lists the company headquarters' mailing address as well as its officers.)

Now's the Time to Mention Your Value

As I said earlier, most customer service reps want to get you off the phone as quickly as possible—they don't particularly care that you're a Very Important Customer. But those higher up in the corporate food chain might. You definitely don't want to start with some declaration like "I'll never shop here again!" (If you've already decided not to come back, why should the company try to accommodate you?) A better approach is to briefly mention any pertinent facts that will establish your value, such as the amount you've already spent with the company; the amounts you were planning to spend in the future; or, if the dollar amounts aren't particularly impressive, just the fact that you're a regular customer and want to continue being one.

Get Help

If none of that works, consider enlisting others who can intervene. Those folks might include state regulators, a consumer advocacy group, a local journalist, or even a lawyer. Although a dispute typically has to be pretty large in financial terms to make a lawsuit worthwhile, sometimes all it takes is a tersely worded letter on an attorney's letterhead to finally get a company's attention.

Your Checklist

Here's your list of things to do from this chapter.

Create your consumer toolkit.

- ☑ Sign up for access to *Consumer Reports'* Web site.

- ☑ Add price comparison sites to your browser's "favorites" list.

- ☑ Install a firewall, antivirus, and antispyware software, and keep them updated.

- ☑ Run antivirus and antispyware scans once a week.

- ☑ Use only secure sites when buying on the Web.

Become a savvier traveler.

- ☑ Concentrate your travel with one airline, one or two hotel chains, and one or two car rental companies, and sign up for their frequent traveler programs.

- ☑ Use third-party travel sites to compare prices and look for vacation packages.

- ☑ Check back to see if travel prices have dropped, and rebook as necessary.

Be a more effective complainer.

- ☑ Know your rights.

- ☑ Know what you want—be concise and reasonable.

- ☑ Use GetHuman.com or use the company's Web site resources to skip voice mail hell.

- ☑ Write a letter to the company's CEO.

- ☑ When all else fails, get outside help.

10

Changing Your
Uneasy Mind

She was writing me, ostensibly, about how big her emergency fund should be. But her anxiety about money was overwhelming: "If I am laid off and use my emergency fund for living expenses, [another] emergency such as a furnace breaking or a car accident could still ruin me financially. I think of this every day, and even though I have over $37,000 in various savings accounts, I still feel like I am close to financial ruin. I don't feel that I have enough, even though my monthly expenses are about $3,000 and I make $75,000 a year."

Another reader was a single mom with two kids who was struggling with big medical bills, collections for old debts, and a budget that never seemed to work. Her mother had already bailed her out once by lending her $15,000 to pay off credit card debt, but she was in financial trouble again.

"I should note that I have spending issues as well that get worse when I feel lost," she wrote, "and right now I feel really lost."

A third reader constantly battled with his wife about money. He made a decent income, but she wanted him to work more hours or switch jobs for higher pay. He already felt like he was on a treadmill, making money that was spent before his paycheck even arrived. He had no hope that making more would solve the problem—he felt that it would just fuel more spending. "Is this a life?" he asked rhetorically.

Money is clearly more than just a means of paying our bills, protecting our families, and providing for our futures. It's also a source of anxiety, fear, and frustration. Many people find themselves stuck dealing with the same issues over and over again. Others start to move forward, only to sabotage their progress with destructive behavior. Still others actually solve their most pressing financial issues but still find themselves worrying that they won't have enough.

Sometimes, in other words, our money problems aren't just in our wallets. They're also in our heads.

In this chapter, you'll find some of the attitudes about money that tend to cause a lot of unnecessary stress. Confronting these misconceptions and replacing them with more accurate perceptions can go a long way toward defusing your money anxieties.

Let me be clear here: I'm not talking about magical thinking, which is the idea that you can change outside reality with the "right" thoughts (and without any other effort on your part). I'm talking about positive, realistic thinking, which is the basis for all constructive change. If you understand how money really works and believe you can apply those principles in your life, you're on your way to an easier relationship with money.

Of course, some money issues are so serious and deep-seated that they need a therapist's help to resolve. If you think that might be your situation and you can't dislodge the attitudes that are causing you pain, please consider investing in some professional help. It could be the best money you've ever spent.

Here are some of the attitudes that could be tripping you up.

"The One Who Dies with the Most Toys Wins"

There's no denying that it's fun to get new stuff. But a life that's a relentless cycle of buying, then working to pay for the stuff, then buying more stuff—well, it's pretty empty.

The reality is our actual *needs* are pretty finite: food, shelter, clothing, companionship. Everything else is a *want*—and our wants are endless.

It's the way we're wired as human beings. Every time we buy something new, we get a rush, but, we quickly start taking our new possession for granted. Then we crave something else. Once again, acquiring the new thing makes us feel good—but only temporarily.

British economist Richard Layard called the process of adapting to ever-improving circumstances a *hedonic treadmill*. After experiencing the thrill of acquisition, we quickly return to our baseline level of happiness and start to cast around for something to give us the next high.

The good thing is that we can step off the treadmill if we want. We don't have to give up all our worldly goods or forsake the mall forever, but we do have to recognize our acquisitiveness for what it is most of the time—a passing fancy that won't really make us any happier.

Chapter 11, "Setting Goals, or What Are You Doing the Rest of Your Life?" includes questions you can ask yourself to help you discover what truly will make you happy and allow you to live a life that feels fulfilling. Once you're on the right path, your desire for "stuff" can take its proper place in your life.

"We'd Be Fine If Our Income Was Just a Little Higher"

The illusion that all we need is just a little more money is almost universal. We're convinced that a higher income would give us the breathing room we need to pay off our debt, save for the future, and just be more comfortable.

Unless you're smart about your money, though, your expenses will increase when your income does. Again, it's just human nature. You make that purchase you've been putting off or take out that loan you couldn't quite afford before. Pretty soon, you'll be right back where you started.

If you're not convinced, just think back to every raise or windfall that ever came your way. You might have felt a flush of victory—at last! Your money situation was going to get easier! Then think of how long it took for you to be stressed again about money.

A variation on this theme is "I should be able to live better than this." I hear this complaint most often from people who make a decent income but who blame "the high cost of living" for their money woes.

In reality, our own choices have a powerful impact on how well we live on the money we make. Where we live, what we drive, how we eat, and what we do with our time are all factors in how far our money goes.

If you really want to achieve peace with your money, you'll need to learn to live on what you're making now. Then you can use every increase in your income to better your situation, rather than constantly slipping back to the same state of debt and anxiety.

"I'll Never Have Enough"

Interestingly, this thought plagues two distinctly different money types: hoarders and spenders.

The hoarder is convinced that disaster lies around every corner, so spending money can actually make her feel sick. (I know you spenders are aghast at the very notion, but it happens.) Some hoarders refer to their "inner bag lady"—the personification of the idea that they could wind up on the street if they don't save every dime they can. The hoarder may delay even necessary purchases out of fear, and discretionary purchases may never get made. The idea that money can be enjoyed today, as well as saved for tomorrow, isn't one the hoarder easily grasps.

At the other end of the spectrum are the spenders who see the life—or rather lifestyle—they want receding ever out of their reach. Whatever they have isn't good enough; it must be replaced by better, newer, shinier, more. It's the "most toys" mentality overlaid with a deep feeling of desperation: "I'll never have enough, so I have to grab everything I can." The idea of *not* spending is what can make them feel sick—gratification delayed is gratification denied forever, in their view.

Sometimes, the conviction that you'll never have enough is so deeply ingrained that only therapy can fully address it. But sometimes just doing a little worst-case scenario brainstorming can snap you back to reality.

After all, total financial wipeouts are still fairly rare, and we do live in an age with safety nets, however tattered they might have become. So the hoarder might ask herself, "What if I did lose all my money tomorrow? What could I do? Who could I turn to? How would I cope? What good things would remain in my life? What nonfinancial assets would I still possess that could help me rebuild?" Realizing she has the strength to handle the worst can help her ease her grip.

Likewise, there will always be people richer, as well as poorer, than we are. So the spender might ask herself, "What if I never do have enough money to buy everything I want? Will my life still have been worth living? What good things would remain in my life? What nonfinancial assets do I possess, regardless of what my material possessions might be?"

If these types can unplug from the idea that money can buy happiness or security, they can make huge progress in their financial and emotional lives.

"I'm Such a Loser; I'd Be So Much Farther Ahead If I Hadn't Made So Many Mistakes with Money"

News flash: *Everybody* makes mistakes with money. Everybody.

Maybe your mistakes cost you a house, or a job, or your retirement fund. Maybe you've wound up in bankruptcy court—perhaps more than once. Or maybe you're just beating yourself up over stupid decisions that cost you money you really couldn't afford to lose.

Yet people bounce back from devastating financial failures all the time. The list of folks who filed for bankruptcy and then went on to greater fame and fortune is a long one and includes Mark Twain, Walt Disney, Donald Trump (a two-time filer, so far), and Wayne Newton.

Perhaps your missteps weren't quite so large, but you still can't forgive yourself for them. Maybe understanding you have plenty of company will help.

One of my favorite discussions on MSN's Your Money message board started when one of the people posting messages decided to confess the stupidest money moves she'd ever made. (Message boards are a kind of online discussion forum, where people type in questions and comments for each other to see.) Pretty soon, everybody started chipping in with their big goofs, which ranged all over the map—from lending money to lovers who disappeared to spending thousands on fitness equipment that turned into glorified clothes racks to losing tens of thousands of dollars on really dumb investments.

People lament the stupid car accidents that cost them bundles, the rebates they never applied for, the small fortunes they waste on stuff that broke or fell apart or they never even used.

I contributed one of my own whoppers, which was buying raw land in Alaska as (get this) retirement property. I was in my 20s and actually thought I could predict where I'd want to live 40 years in the future. And I'm talking really raw land: there wasn't—and isn't to this day—a road within 80 miles. I financed this brilliant purchase at 12 percent interest for several years, only to decide, right about the time I paid it off, that I'd had enough of cold weather, whereupon I decamped to California. Of course, I couldn't find a buyer, then or now, so this lovely little piece of ridiculously remote acreage is still mine.

The thing is, many, if not most, of the people who posted comments on the MSN Web site are pretty smart (at least now) about money. They're saving for retirement, they have emergency funds, they don't carry credit card debt, and they have their finances in pretty good order.

The difference between smart people and not-so-smart ones is that the smart people *learn* from their mistakes and try to do better the next time. You'll still make mistakes, of course, but as you grow in wealth and understanding, those mistakes are likely to be ones you can recover from fairly quickly.

"I'll Never Understand This Money Stuff"

Some of the brightest people I know are convinced that money is some kind of mysterious, complex rocket science that's entirely beyond them. One friend confessed that whenever I answered her questions about personal finance, my words turned to the "wah wah wah" background noise that adults make in old Charlie Brown cartoons.

"I'm really trying to listen," she said. "I just can't hear the words."

There are some areas of money that are pretty arcane. Derivatives and the inner workings of hedge funds, for example, can be pretty complex. But most of what you need to know about money is relatively straightforward. You don't need to be a rocket scientist to learn about money, although you might have to persevere a bit if you get confused.

In fact, if you're smart enough to read this book, you're smart enough to get your finances under control. Just keep reading, listening, and asking questions, and pretty soon the "wah wah wah" will start to make sense.

"It's Not My Fault"

This is actually one of the most destructive money attitudes of all.

It's tempting, when things go wrong, to want to blame other people or "the system" for giving you a raw deal. Maybe your ex skipped out and left you a pile of debt, or you're having trouble finding work in your field, or you've been hit by health problems or disability and didn't have enough insurance.

Life isn't always fair. Lots of people have gotten truly raw deals. But if you let the reasons for your financial troubles harden into excuses—if, in other words, you decide to be a permanent victim and not look for a solution—the one who suffers is you.

Perhaps you couldn't avoid the catastrophe that befell you. But it's still up to you to figure out how to pick up the pieces and move on.

And maybe you had more of a role in your current situation than you'd like to admit. In one of my columns for MSN Money, I suggested the following exercise for those who are convinced their money problems are someone else's fault:

- **Write down your five most pressing money concerns**—Is it credit card debt? A rising mortgage payment? A budget that doesn't balance? Inadequate retirement savings? Whatever your big money troubles, put them in writing.

- **Determine your role, if any**—What choices did you make
  that either helped put you in this position or made matters
  worse? Did you

  - Spend more than you made?

  - Fail to have a rainy-day fund?

  - Try to get by with too little insurance?

  - Fail to pay attention to the terms of the loan you were
    getting?

  - Figure "something will work out" rather than having
    a plan?

  - Procrastinate on dealing with an issue until it became a big
    problem?

This part of the exercise isn't designed to make you feel bad or stupid. Rather,
it's to help you realize that you may have a role in creating your financial situation—and you certainly have a role in finding a solution. Rather than being
a powerless victim, you can be empowered to fix your situation. To that end:

- **Brainstorm some solutions**—Temporarily ban the words
  can't, *won't*, and *but* (as in "I can't do that," "That won't
  work," and "Yeah, but…"). Instead, think of every solution
  you can. No idea is too wild to at least consider. If you need
  help, consider posting your money problems on the Your
  Money message board on MSN.com. There you can tap into
  the expertise of hundreds of other readers who have faced and
  solved similar dilemmas. Then make a plan to fix the mess
  and follow through.

What if you're convinced that your problem is your partner or spouse, and she
won't cooperate in a solution?

Finger-pointing is particularly devastating in committed relationships,
and few financial problems are entirely one person's fault. Typically, both
partners have contributed to the problem, according to Olivia Mellan, a
money therapist and author of the terrific book *Overcoming Overspending: A
Winning Plan for Spenders and Their Partners*. If you think your spouse is a
spendthrift, for example, you may clamp down and start treating her like a

wayward child. This may prompt your spouse to rebel and spend even more. The cycle can persist until you wind up in bankruptcy or divorce court—or both.

If your union and your finances are to survive, you'll have to work out compromises. If you can't do it on your own, a trained therapist can help.

Money and Your Brain

It makes sense that money problems can cause emotional and mental problems, leading to stress, anxiety, and even depression.

What you may not know is that money problems also can be a *symptom* of some common mental disorders:

- The manic or "high" phase of manic-depression, also known as bi-polar disorder, is often characterized by impulsivity, which can result in huge, budget-destroying spending sprees.

- People who are depressed can overspend in an attempt to alleviate their mood, or they may neglect their personal finances because they feel so hopeless about the future.

- Adults with attention deficit/hyperactivity disorder (ADHD) may also have trouble managing their finances for a variety of reasons. Problems with impulse control can lead to overspending; while trouble planning, organizing, or dealing with mundane details can make even relatively simple tasks, such as paying bills, seem impossible.

- People with addictions—to drugs, alcohol, gambling, or anything else—often leave their finances in tatters.

If you suspect that your money problems may be a symptom of a deeper mental health issue, spend some time educating yourself about these conditions and consider seeking an evaluation by a mental health professional. Treatment, including medication and/or therapy, might be indicated.

Discovering that your money problems are related to mental problems doesn't exactly let you off the hook for creating financial chaos in your life. You'll still have to deal with the wreckage you've created and figure out better ways to handle your money in the future. But if your brain is wired differently from most folks, it can help to understand that and take compensatory action.

For more information about:

- **Depression and Bipolar Disorder**—Check out the Depression and Bipolar Support Alliance at www.ndmda.org.

- **ADHD**—See the Attention Deficit Disorder Alliance at www.add.org.

- **Addictions**—Visit the Web sites for Alcoholics Anonymous at www.alcoholics-anonymous.org, Narcotics Anonymous at www.na.org, Gamblers Anonymous at www.gamblersanonymous.org or Debtors Anonymous at http://debtorsanonymous.org.

Your Checklist

Here's your list of things to do from this chapter.

☑ Write down some of the attitudes or thoughts about money that cause you to be uneasy.

☑ Now counter those sentiments: write down a more positive attitude or constructive thought. Consult your counterarguments when you're troubled by money worries.

☑ If you're not clear about your responsibility for your money future, do the exercise described in "It's Not My Fault."

☑ If your money problems persist, your fears are overwhelming, or you suspect an underlying mental disorder or addiction, get help. A trained therapist can help you with individual counseling, while 12-step groups provide support and help for free.

11

Setting Goals, Or What Are You Doing the Rest of Your Life?

Many books on personal finance put the "goal setting" chapter at the very front. The idea is that if you don't know exactly where you're going, you're likely to wind up somewhere else.

True enough. But I think you need to have a clear picture of where you are and get some of the niggling details of your finances resolved before you can take a deep breath and figure out where you want to go next.

Let's start with a fun little exercise involving the benefits estimate that the Social Security Administration sends you every year about three months before your birthday. (If you lost your last one, you can request a replacement at the Social Security Administration site, www.socialsecurity.gov/statement/, or by calling 800-772-1213.)

The benefits estimate not only shows what you're supposed to receive from Social Security when you retire, but it also includes a lifetime record of your earnings. That's what we're after.

What I want you to do is add up the figures to see how much money you've earned so far during your life.

There are typically two columns of figures, one for "Social Security earnings" and one for "Medicare earnings." If the figures are different, which they may be if you're a big earner, use the Medicare column.

Now think about any other income you've received in your life that wasn't reported as wages to the Social Security Administration. That could include babysitting and odd jobs you did when you were young and money you earned "under the table," as well as gifts of money, inheritances, alimony, and child support. Precision isn't essential; just make your best guess.

Income Source	Amount
Lifetime earnings (from SSA statement)	
Off-the-books earnings	
Money gifts	
Inheritances	
Alimony	
Child support	
Other	
Total:	

Once you've done that, I'll want you to tote up your net worth. Start by writing down the fair market value of your assets: what your home, cars, and other possessions would be worth if you sold them today.

Then total what you owe in loans: mortgages, auto loans, student loans, credit card debt, and so on.

Your financial net worth is the total of what you own, minus what you owe.

Assets	Value
Home	
Other real estate	
Cars	
Other vehicles	
Jewelry	
Furniture/household	
Checking/savings accounts	
Retirement accounts	
Brokerage accounts	
Savings bonds/CDs	
Stocks/mutual funds	
Life insurance (cash value)	
Other	

Liabilities	Principal Owed
Mortgage	
Home equity loan	
Other real estate loans	
Car loans	
Student loans	
Credit card debt	
Other loans	
Net Worth:	

Now compare your financial net worth to your total lifetime income figure.

The ratio might not be impressive. If you're young—in your 20s, say—the net worth-to-income ratio is probably 10 percent or less; if it's 25 percent, you're doing well. As you approach retirement, the ratio should be substantially higher—I'd hope for 100 percent or more, although people can get by with less.

The point of this exercise isn't really to benchmark yourself. It's to see, in precise dollar terms, how much wealth you've created from the money that has entered your life.

Of course, money has more uses than simply building up a treasure chest. We also use it to pay other important, life-enhancing things.

Some of my own expenditures were investments in real-dollar terms, even though I wasn't buying houses or stocks. I helped pay for my college education and went to night school in my 30s to study financial planning, for example, both big investments in my future earning power.

But a lot of our best spending creates nothing but memories and connections. My list of highlights encompasses extensive travel, including trips to Europe and India; visits with family, including two sabbaticals from work that allowed me to care for my dying mother; flying lessons to earn a pilot's license; some memorable parties; charitable donations; and financial gifts to struggling family members. Now that we have a child, a lot of money goes to her care and education (plus more than a few princess costumes).

Think for a moment about what your money has bought you. What experiences have you had? What memories have you created? What's the best money you ever spent? Take some time to write out a list that includes every expenditure you can remember that you're glad you made.

These are our life assets, and we want to build these up at the same time that we're increasing our financial wealth.

To help you figure out how to do that, I'm going to rely heavily on the groundbreaking work of financial planner George Kinder, who wrote *The Seven Stages of Money Maturity: Understanding the Spirit and Value of Money in Your Life* and who is considered one of the founders of the "life planning" movement.

Those who practice life planning say they're looking for a more holistic approach to financial planning. They try to discover and implement their clients' most deeply held values instead of concentrating just on accumulating a big pile of money.

Visualizing Your Ideal Life

To help uncover these values, Kinder asks his clients to first imagine that they've already achieved financial security. Perhaps they've retired or received an inheritance that meant they no longer had to work. They now have enough money to take care of all their needs for the rest of their lives. If that were the case, Kinder asks them, how would they live their lives? What would they do with their time and their money? Would they change anything about their lives?

I'd encourage you to take a moment to imagine yourself in this scenario. Close your eyes and visualize, in the greatest detail you can, the life you would lead if lack of money were no longer an issue. Then *write down* the answers to Kinder's questions.

Consider dedicating a notebook to this exercise, or if you prefer using a computer, a separate folder on your desktop. The act of writing is an important part of this process. It helps you focus your thoughts and gives you something concrete to refer to later.

This exercise may take you a while, and that's fine. Write as much as you can and then come back to the book when you're done.

Finished? Let's move on to the next set of questions.

Setting the Timer

After his clients have visualized and detailed their ideal life, Kinder presents them with another scenario. Visualize yourself in your current life, only now you're sitting in your doctor's office. You've just been told that you have 5 to

10 years to live. You'll be healthy until the moment you die, but you'll have no advance notice of exactly when your time is up.

Now answer these questions, again in writing.

- What will you do in the time you have remaining to live?

- Will you change your life?

- If so, how will you change it?

Do this now and then come back to the book when you're done.

The End Game

For the last group of questions, visualize yourself back in the doctor's office. There's been a mistake. Instead of 5 to 10 years, you learn you have a single day to live. As you absorb this news, pay attention to the feelings that arise as you confront your own impending death.

Heavy, right? But this step is crucial. Now answer these four final questions.

- Which of your dreams will be left unfulfilled?

- What do you wish you had finished or had been?

- What do you wish you had done?

- What did you miss?

Spend some time exploring these questions. Write down your honest responses. Don't judge—just express what you really feel.

What It's All About

Every time I do these exercises, I discover something fairly profound about my goals, my values, and what I want out of life—some core value that I'd been neglecting or pushing away surfaces to demand attention.

The first time I did them, I was a daily newspaper reporter desperate for more control over my time and my life. I visualized a life working from home writing columns, rather than breaking news stories. When an opportunity to do just that arose, I was able to put my fears aside and grab it.

I also uncovered a desire to become a mom—something that had been pushed aside in my daily fight to meet deadlines and earn a living. Hubby and I got serious and got busy, and the result—our daughter—brings daily joy into our life.

Kinder's questions are designed to help you drill down to what's really important to you. Once you've identified these core values, you can start incorporating them in your life.

One woman I interviewed discovered that she was basically pretty happy with the life she had and where she was going. But she uncovered a deep desire to help other people, from struggling family members to children in underdeveloped countries. This knowledge led her to set up education funds for her nieces and nephews and to sponsor children through an international charitable program.

Of course, you may discover more profound changes are needed.

Maybe you've been focused on advancing your career and earning more money. But in this exercise, you realize that what you really want is more time, right now, with your young children. You may decide to throttle back on the job or even switch careers to give you more time with the people who matter.

Or you may find that your goal of financial independence is so important to you that you're willing to make big changes to achieve it, like moving to a cheaper area of the country or taking on a second job so you can get out of debt.

Kinder tells the story of a successful doctor who wanted, deep down, to be a rabbi. The doctor thought he could make the change in 10 or 15 years, after his four kids were educated and out of the house. Kinder challenged him to make the change in two years, and the doctor ultimately did it in four, thanks to the support of his family. They moved from their swanky house to a less expensive neighborhood, changed their spending habits, and were rewarded with a dad who was not only happier but who had more time for his family.

Sometimes it takes real work and struggle to figure out how to change your life to reflect your core values. Coordinating your dreams with those of a partner can be even more challenging. Try fantasizing all kinds of different solutions before you narrow your options to the ones that will get you where you want to be the quickest.

Once again, you'll need to remove *can't*, *won't*, and *yeah, but* from your vocabulary. You'll obviously need to identify the obstacles that stand in your way, but don't stop there. Keep zeroing in on solutions.

Here are some more questions to ask yourself.

• What's standing between me and what I want?

• What's my plan for overcoming each of these obstacles?

• What do I have, in terms of personal strengths and outside resources, that will help me deal with these obstacles?

• What skills and knowledge do I need to add to accomplish this change?

• Are there other people I can call on for help in overcoming these obstacles?

• What's my time line for overcoming these obstacles?

• How can I make these changes happen sooner?

• Do I need my family's support for making this change?

• If so, how can I rally that support?

• How can I evaluate and monitor my progress toward my goals?

Again, it's important to write down your answers using as many pages as necessary until you form a coherent plan. Then go ahead and set yourself some deadlines. Put them on your calendar. Keep evaluating your progress.

This is the one life you get. Make sure you get what you really want.

Previous chapters ended with checklists to help you organize and streamline your financial life. I'll end the book a little differently with just one more exercise to do—and that's to write yourself a letter summarizing what you've learned about yourself and your money using the exercises in this chapter. Describe the values you've discovered and outline the changes you want to make in your life. Then, tuck this letter away somewhere safe and make a note on your calendar to check it again in six months. See how far you've come and what you've changed. If you want to share the results with me—and I hope you will—just use the "Contact Liz" tab on my Web site (www.asklizweston.com). I look forward to hearing from you.

Resources and Recommendations

There are thousands of books and Web sites that want to teach you about money. I've winnowed out a relative handful that deserve space on your bookshelf or on the "favorites" tab of your browser.

The Basics

Your Money or Your Life: Transforming Your Relationship with Money and Achieving Financial Independence by **Joe Dominguez and Vicki Robin**—Written in 1992, this best-seller has been translated into nine languages and remains the bible of the voluntary simplicity movement. You don't need to be on that particular path, however, to benefit enormously from the principles in this book.

Personal Finance for Dummies, **5th Edition by Eric Tyson**—Tyson's book is probably the best all-around primer for anyone who wants to learn about money.

The Richest Man in Babylon by **George Clason**—Written as a parable in 1927, it contains timeless instruction on achieving financial success.

College

The Best Way to Save for College 2007: A Complete Guide to 529 Plans by **Joseph F. Hurley**—Hurley is the go-to guy on college savings plans, and he also has good information on Coverdells. His SavingForCollege.com site is well worth bookmarking, as is his "World's Simplest College Cost Calculator," which you'll find at:

http://www.savingforcollege.com/college-savings-calculator/

FinAid.org (www.finaid.org)—As its name suggests, this site focuses on financial aid. Its Expected Family Contribution Calculator is especially helpful for those who will be navigating the financial aid maze:

http://www.finaid.org/calculators/finaidestimate.phtml

Couples & Money

Smart Couples Finish Rich: 9 Steps to Creating a Rich Future for You and Your Partner **by David Bach**—Bach's best-seller is a helpful guide to navigating your financial future with a partner.

Overcoming Overspending: A Winning Plan for Spenders and Their Partners **by Olivia Mellan**—Mellan is a therapist who specializes in financial issues, and her book is the best I've ever seen on dealing with compulsive spenders.

Credit & Debt

Your Credit Score: How to Fix, Improve, and Protect the 3-Digit Number that Shapes Your Financial Future, **Second Edition by Liz Pulliam Weston**—Yes, I'm touting my own book, but I believe it's the best available on the intricacies of credit scoring.

Deal with Your Debt: The Right Way to Manage Your Bills and Pay Off What You Owe **by Liz Pulliam Weston**—I'm doing it again, but if you want a sensible approach to paying off debt, you'll find it here.

Solve Your Money Troubles: Get Debt Collectors Off Your Back & Regain Financial Freedom, **Eleventh Edition by Robin Leonard and John Lamb**—At last, a book by somebody else. If you're really over your head, grab this life preserver of a book and start reading.

Bankrate.com (www.bankrate.com)—This site is packed with information about saving, credit, and debt. Among its many great tools is its FICO score estimator:

http://www.bankrate.com/brm/fico/calc.asp

CardRatings.com (www.cardratings.com)—A good, comprehensive, free site that can help you find and compare credit card offers. The articles and tools can help you be a smarter credit consumer.

National Foundation for Credit Counseling (www.nfcc.org)—This is the oldest and most-respected credit counseling organization. If you're behind on your bills and want to try to avoid bankruptcy, consider a consultation with one of its affiliated agencies.

Estate Planning

Plan Your Estate by **Denis Clifford and Cora Jordan**—Estate planning is an immensely complicated topic and, in my view, a dangerous place for novices to tread. But this clear, readable, and comprehensive book serves as a good primer for those who want to do it themselves and those who just want to figure out what the heck their lawyers are saying.

Investing

AnnuityTruth (www.annuitytruth.org)—Are you an older person contemplating buying an annuity? Before you sign on the dotted line, check out this Web site operated by H.E.L.P., a non-profit organization dedicated to educating older Americans about financial issues.

The Little Book of Common Sense Investing: The Only Way to Guarantee Your Fair Share of Stock Market Returns by **John Bogle**—If you don't have time to read Burton G. Malkiel's weighty *A Random Walk Down Wall Street*, Vanguard Funds founder Bogle has written the condensed version.

Real Estate

The Fearless Home Seller: Razzi's Rules for Staying in Control of the Deal
by Elizabeth Razzi—Even folks who have sold a few homes can learn a lot
from Elizabeth Razzi, who wrote about real estate for a decade at Kiplinger's
personal finance magazine.

100 Questions Every First-Time Home Buyer Should Ask **by Ilyce Glink**—
Glink has written several excellent books about money and real estate, and
this one guides first-timers through an often harrowing process.

**HUD-approved housing counselors (http://www.hud.gov/offices/hsg/sfh/
hcc/hcs.cfm)**—Counselors approved by the U.S. Housing and Urban
Development Department can offer consumer-friendly advice on buying a
home, renting, defaults, foreclosures, credit issues, and reverse mortgages.

Retirement

*Saving for Retirement (Without Living Like a Pauper or Winning the
Lottery)* **by Gail MarksJarvis**—MarksJarvis, an award-winning *Chicago
Tribune* columnist, offers a readable guide that covers the basics of retirement
investing.

Get a Life: You Don't Need a Million to Retire Well **by Ralph E. Warner**—
Technically, this is a book about retirement, but its real message is the importance of having a balanced approach to money.

IRAs, 401ks, & Other Retirement Plans: Taking Your Money Out **by Twila
Slesnick and John C. Suttle**—Before you crack your nest egg—prematurely
or in preparation for retirement—read this book. You'll still want to talk to a
tax pro, but at least you'll know the questions to ask.

MSN Money (http://money.msn.com)—This site (for which I write a twice-
weekly column) is packed with great financial information and tools, but its
retirement information is particularly helpful. Make sure to check out the
Retirement Planner to see if you're on track with your investments:

http://moneycentral.msn.com/retire/planner.aspx

Savings Tips

The Dollar Stretcher (www.stretcher.com)—Publisher Gary Foreman, a former Certified Financial Planner, was running a "Web 2.0" community-fueled site many, many years before it became the latest Internet trend. Much of the content here is contributed by readers, and you can't beat the extensive library of tips and suggestions for stretching a buck.

Tiptionary 2: Save Time and Money Every Day with 2,300 All-New Tips **by Mary Hunt**—Hunt, who runs the Debt-Proof Living Web site, is the author of several excellent books on saving money. Her latest is packed with ways to live your life better for less.

The Complete Tightwad Gazette **by Amy Dacyczyn**—This weighty book, published nearly 10 years ago, is still the most comprehensive guide to trimming virtually every expense in your life.

INDEX

padding, 5-6
savings accounts
emergency funds, 30
high-yield savings
accounts, 6-7
Bankrate.com, 177
bankruptcy, 53
bargain-hunting
sites, 148-150
Ben's Bargains, 149
The Best Way to Save
for College 2007: A
Complete Guide to
529 Plans, **175**
bills, paying
alerts, 11
bill calendars, 9
checklist of monthly
bills, 9
customizing due dates, 11
e-bills/e-statements, 12
electronic payments
advantages of, 12-13
automatic credit card
charges, 15
automatic debits, 15
choosing best payment
method, 15
online bill pay, 14
security, 13-14
Bogle, John, 66
bonds, 67-68
bounced checks, avoiding
overdraft protection, 4-5
padding accounts, 5-6

brokerage accounts
linking to other accounts, 4
online access, 4
budgets
buy-nothing months, 36-37
determining how much
income to count, 31
determining how much you
can spend, 38-39
emergency funds, 30
50/30/20 plan, 31-38
overview, 27-28
planning for
homeownerships, 120-121
prioritizing goals, 39-41
60 percent solution, 28-31
Buffett, Warren, 66
buy-nothing months, 36-37
buying
automobiles
auto leases, 131
dangers of
overspending, 128-132
depreciation, 131
refinancing, 132
repossession, 132
researching, 132
homes
advantages/disadvantages,
117-119
budgets, 120-121
home-buying
timeline, 119-121
mortgages, 121-128

spreadsheets (Excel), 18
Stanley, Debbie, 22
staying up-to-date, 22-23
stock market
average annual returns,
61, 65-66
bonds/cash, 67-68
diversification, 62-64
ETFs (exchange-traded
funds), 63-64
immediate annuities, 83
mutual funds, 63
index funds, 66-67
life-cycle funds, 70
target maturity
funds, 71-72
overview, 61-62
passive management, 63
tax implications, 139
variable annuities, 72
storage, 20
Strategies for Smart Car
Buyers, 132
student loans, 89

T

T. Rowe Price retirement
income calculator, 83
target maturity funds, 71-72
tax tips, 35
tax professionals
choosing, 139-140
when to hire, 138-139
TaxCut, 138
term life insurance, 112

30-year, fixed-rate
mortgages, 122-123
Tiptionary 2: Save Time and
Money Every Day with
2,300 All-New Tips, 179
toolkit
account aggregation, 17-18
account consolidation, 7-8, 18
command center, 20-22
direct deposit, 4
Excel spreadsheets, 18
high-yield savings
accounts, 6-7
linked accounts, 4
online account access, 4
overdraft protection, 4-5
personal finance
software, 16-17
traditional IRAs, 73-74
transportation expenses, 35
travel rewards credit cards, 57
travel tips, 24, 151-152
trusts, living, 143
TurboTax, 138
Tyagi, Amelia Warren, 28

U-V

umbrella liability
insurance, 107
universal default penalties, 48
utility expenses, 35

Vanguard 529 college savings
plans, 93
variable annuities, 72